If I Only Had More Time

IF I ONLY HAD MORE TIME:
A COLLECTION OF PHOTOGRAPHIC POETRY

Marlene Sotelo

To my mother, who taught me how to love, and to Mother Nature for all the beautiful gifts around me that I capture in my photographs and that inspire my poetry.

Table of Contents

Acknowledgements

Photography has been a hobby I have enjoyed for many years. I love capturing moments in time that can last forever and allow me to reflect, contemplate life, and feel gratitude.

The photos collected here reflect moments alone in nature, stopping to capture something worth noting. We are often in such a hurry or looking down at our cellphones that we forget to look up and around to notice the beauty all around us. I am grateful for the many moments I experienced over the years that allowed me to compile this collection of photographic poetry to share with others.

Thank you to my husband, Tony, who bought me a professional camera and encouraged me to get a new cellphone that had a better camera so that I could capture moments anywhere, anytime.

Thank you to my son, Jordan, for inspiring me with his tenacity, dedication, and drive for greatness.

Thank you to my forever friend, Laura, who encouraged me to do something with my photos and poems, and for being there for me through all the highs and all the lows.

Thank you to my siblings, Marisa, Alex, and Michael. We are the POWER OF 4. Our love for each other and for our family is a magnet for all those around us.

Thank you to my mother and father for all the love and care they have given me and my son, Jordan. You are the symbol of love triumphing over all obstacles.

Thank you to my friends for your love over the years: a shoulder to lean on, an ear to listen to, a smile to brighten my day, and ideas shared to keep going strong.

Thank you to all the families of children with autism that I have been privileged to work with over the last 30 years, and to the angels with autism that have given me so much more than I could ever give them.

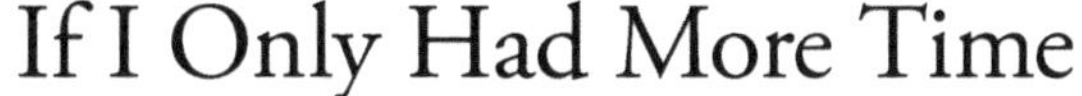

If I Only Had More Time

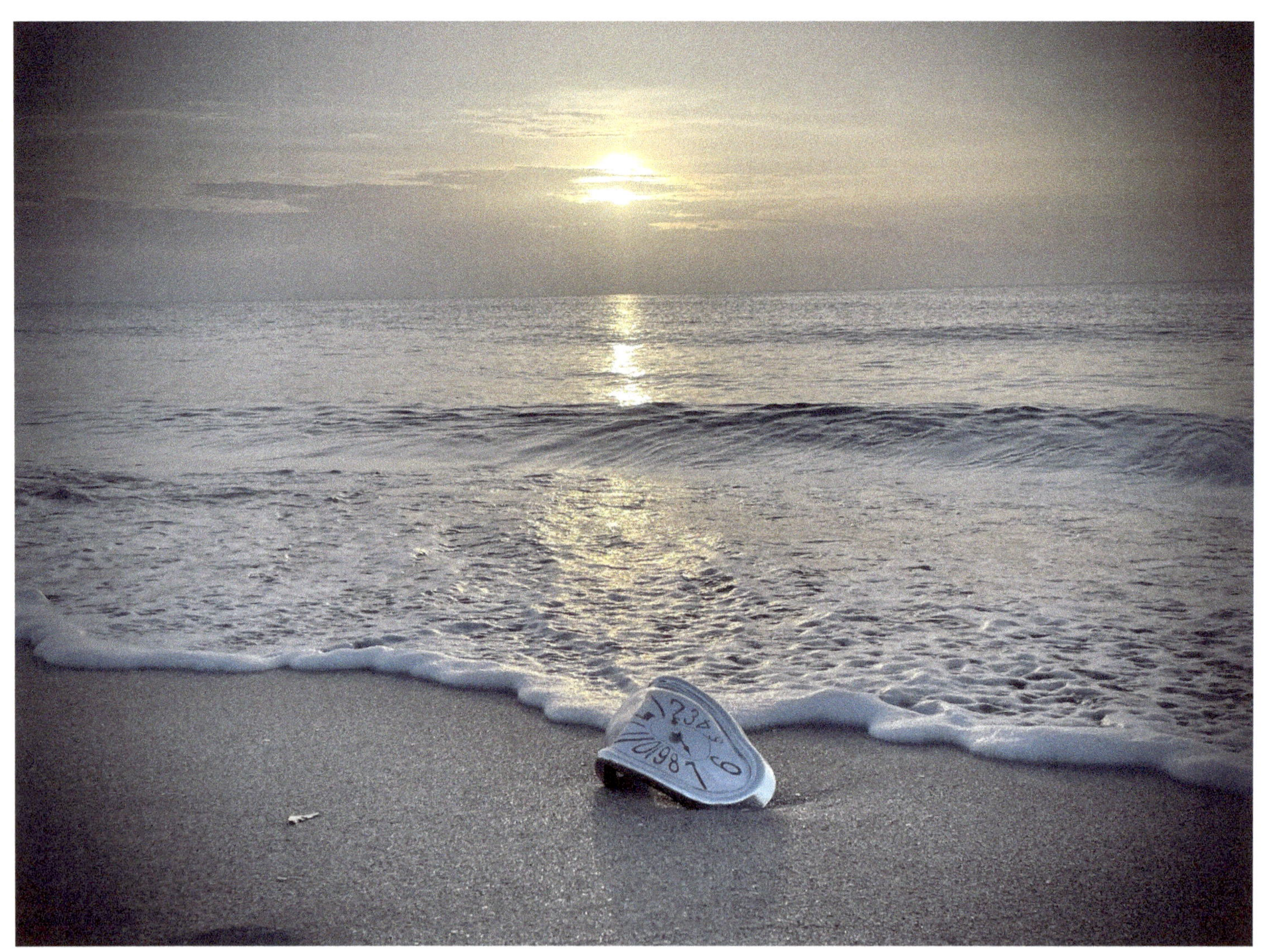

Time

Seconds disappear with the crest of each wave.
Rolling onto the shore bringing new and taking old.
Minutes fly by as the sun appears on the horizon.
As the light of day shines upon us with warm rays of gold.
Hours drag by through the long working day.
Waiting for the moment that I'll be with you holding hands.
Years flash before my eyes remembering the first kiss.
The *Day* time stood still knowing it was you and me together until the end.
Time after time.
As time goes by.
Time in a bottle.
Feels like the first time.
If we only had more time.

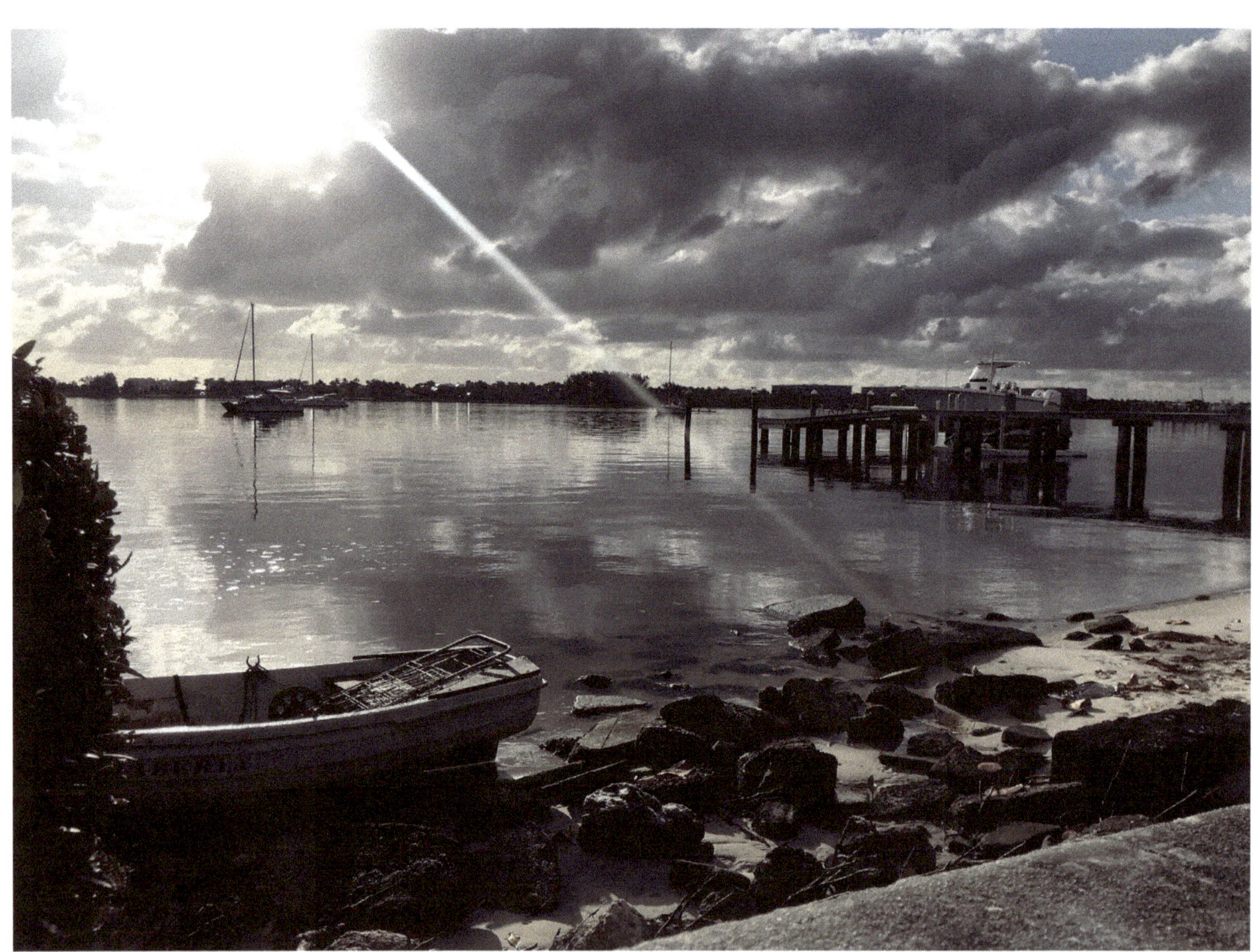

You are Light

Every soul comes into this world pure and ready for a destined journey.
Trials and tribulations mold the person with good and bad as they carve their own path.
Pain and suffering inflicted on others from scars left deep inside, marking the other soul and
pulling you down for reasons one may never know.
But we each have our own journey in life, with free will to choose our own path by our responses to the
actions of others that have nothing to do with our core, with who we are, and who we were meant to be at the
end of the road.
Forgiveness is your key to unlocking the map
that will guide you in your journey to enlightenment.
Forgive not for the other, but instead… for YOU.
You are in control.
You have the power.
You will not let the past stop you from achieving all that your
soul came to this earth to do and all you have to give.
Let go so you can go back to walking the path that you were meant to be in life.
You are love.
You are light.
Always love.

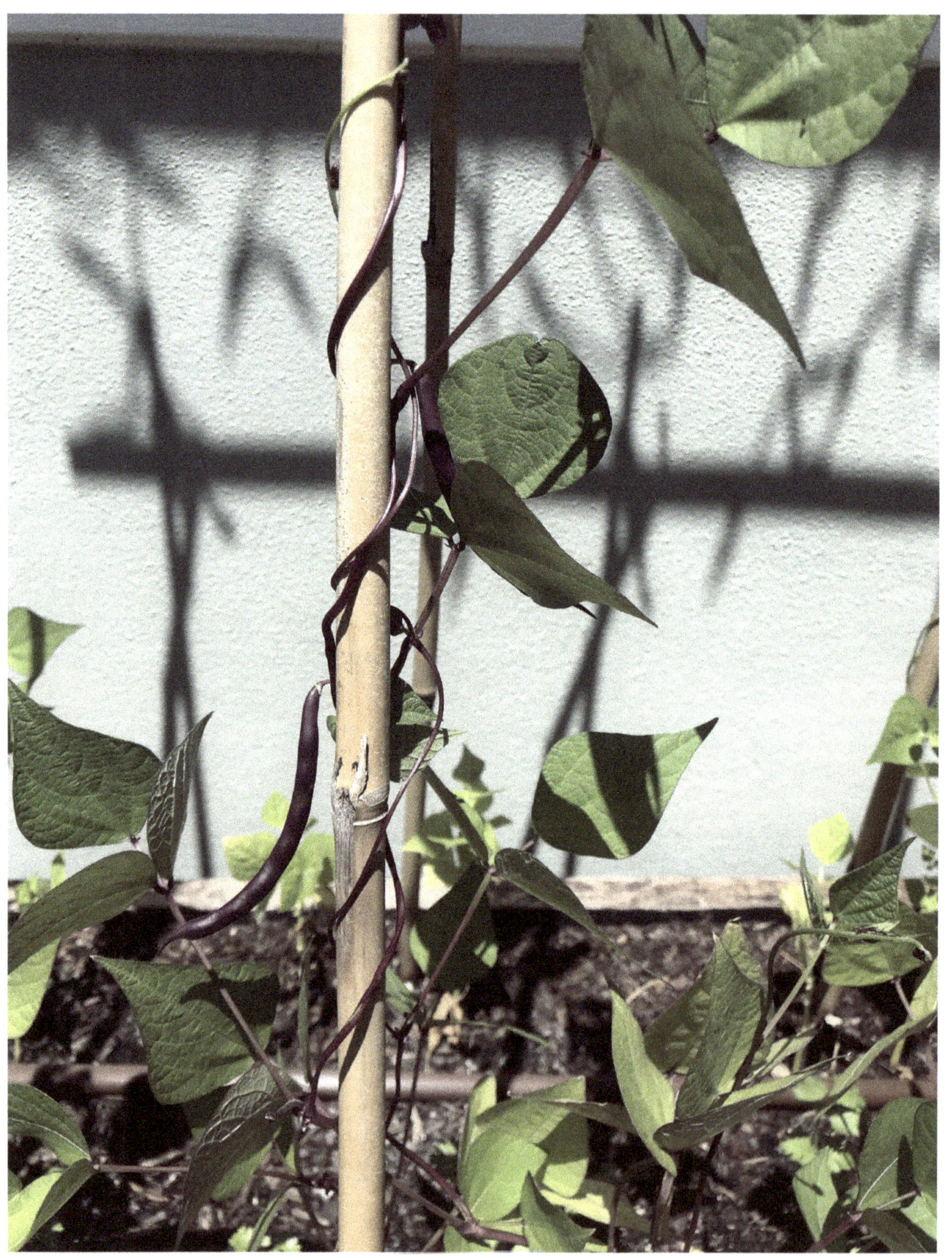

Hope

The seed lies still.
The soil is thrown.
Water poured over,
A future unknown.
The sun shines down,
As roots take hold.
What cannot be seen,
A story yet to be told.
Waiting and wondering,
Will it grow strong and tall,
Or will leaves start to wither,
And branches break and fall.
Pondering the future,
With hands raised above.
Realizing all that is left,
Is unconditional love.

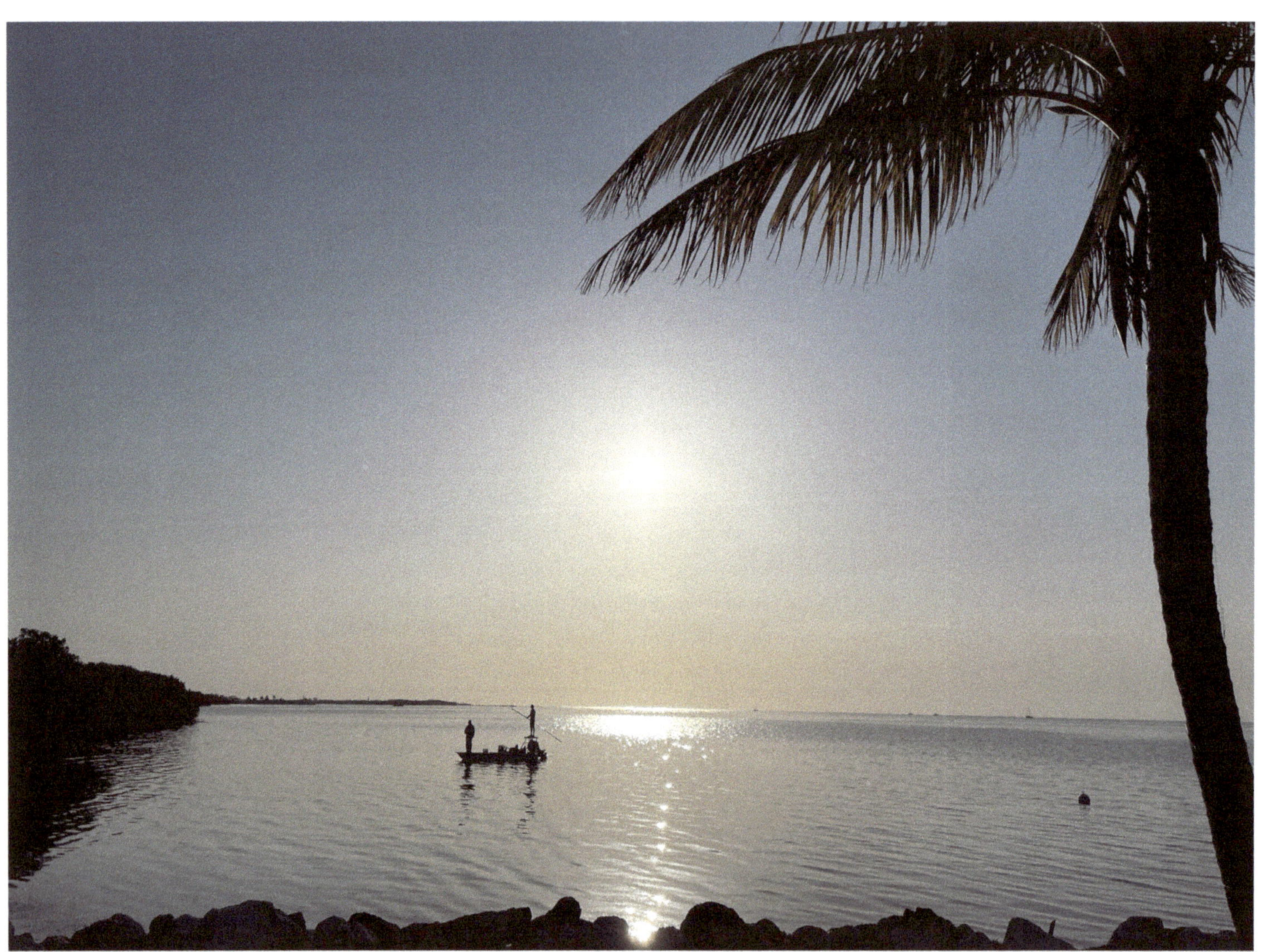

I am Here

I can hear you whisper with your eyes.
Listen to your voice with the touch of your hand.
You pull away, then look away, but I hear you!
Your fears and doubts come rushing through
as you walk past me.
Turning briefly to look my way to see if I'm still there.
I look for answers in your movements, in your smile, and in your touch.
I am here.
I am listening.
I am with you.
For you are me and I am you.

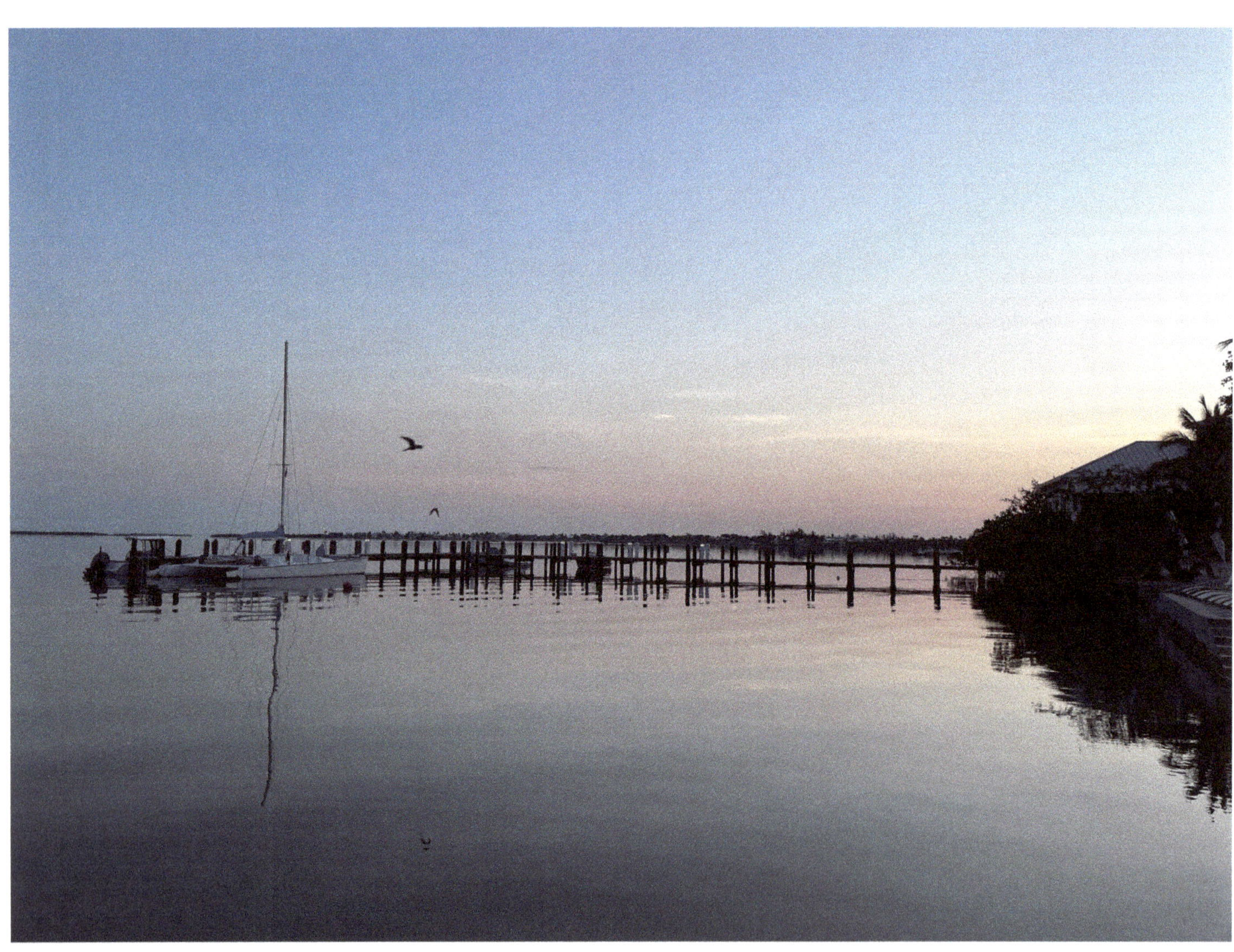

Today is the Day

A speck of dust amongst the stars with meaning to uncover.
Each day gives rise to moments to learn purpose in this cluster.
The why, the how, the what, the when, the questions we all ponder.
At sunset, sunrise, dusk to dawn until one day it is all gone.
Why wait for answers that may never come,
To take this life by storm.
When stars shine bright inside of you, live it before it's gone.

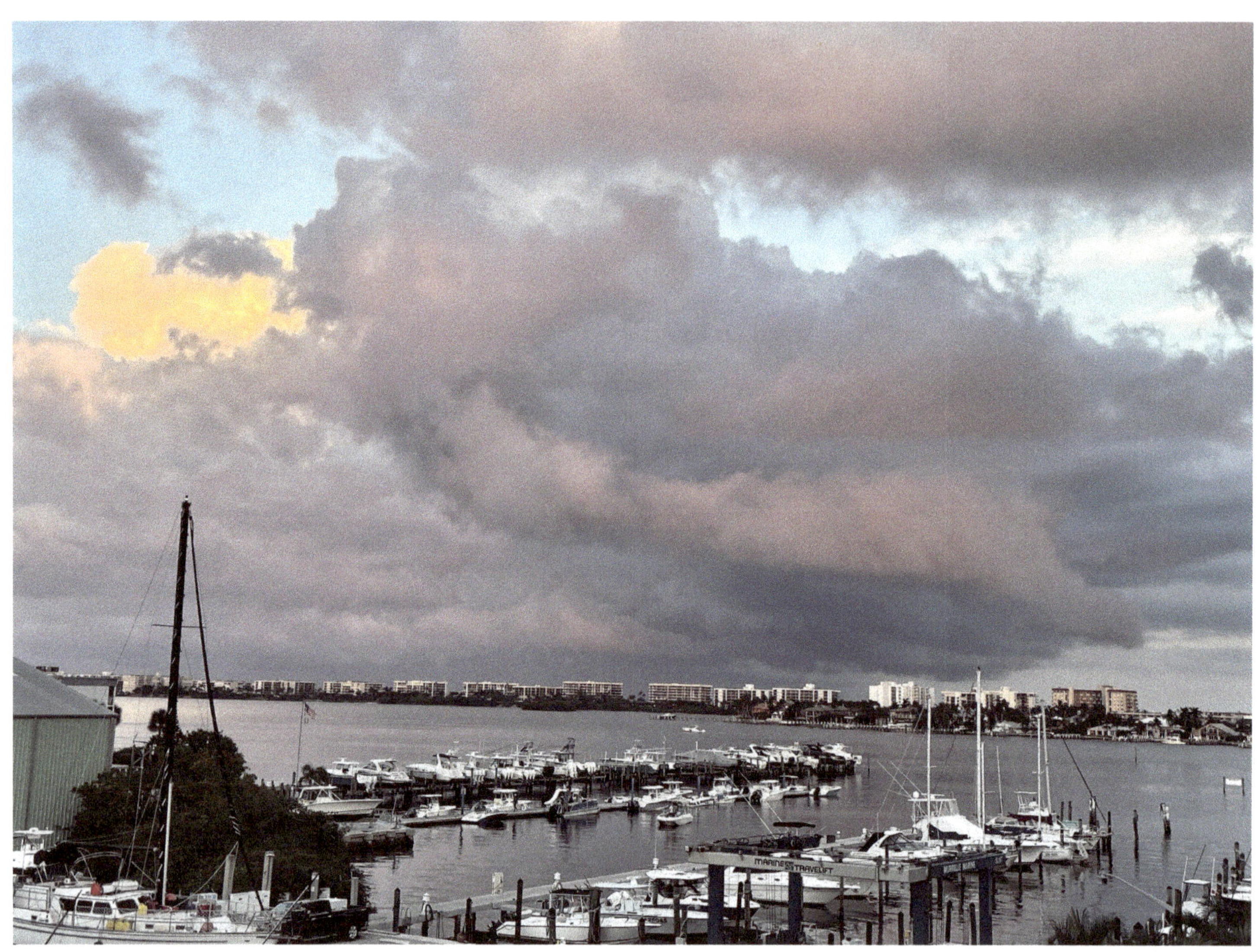

Dark Days

Can you see the light amidst the darkness?
Can you understand the reasons why?
Will the fight for what is right ever be won?
Will the battle to be heard ever be done?
As egos flare and pride takes hold, the ones that need us most, their stories left untold.
When did being good become bad? When did right become wrong?
When did reaching out your hand leave them tied behind your back?
When did helping others leave you alone feeling attacked?
A new day begins, but darkness still lingers.
It grips on your soul from your toes through your fingers.
But for you this moment, right here, right now, let the light bring you peace,
And help you feel content.

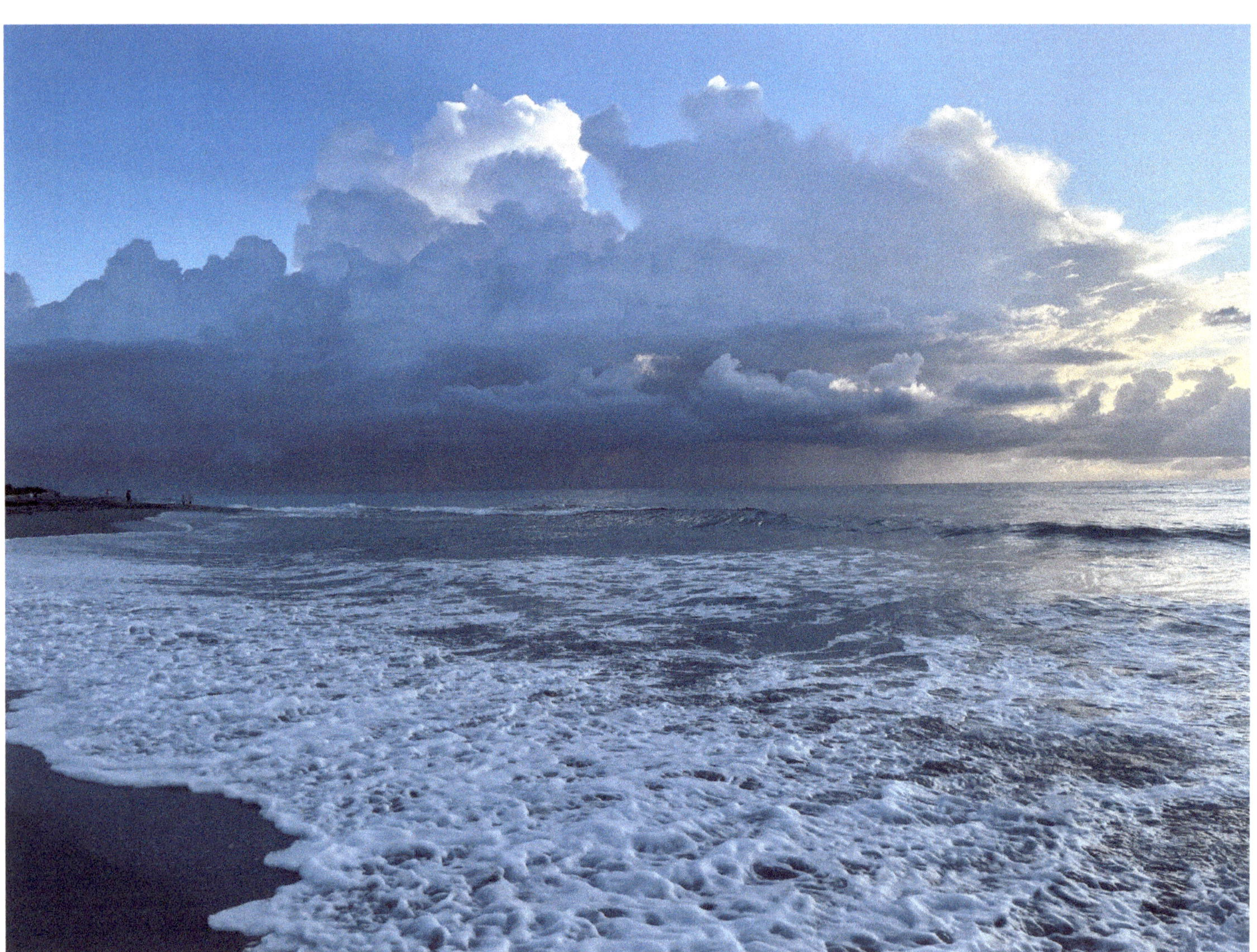

Morning Blues

Morning blues, with a storm in the distance,
Keeping happiness at bay.
Light seeping through like a beacon in the night,
Deepening thoughts pondering which way to go.
Knowing you can decide your existence today and forever.

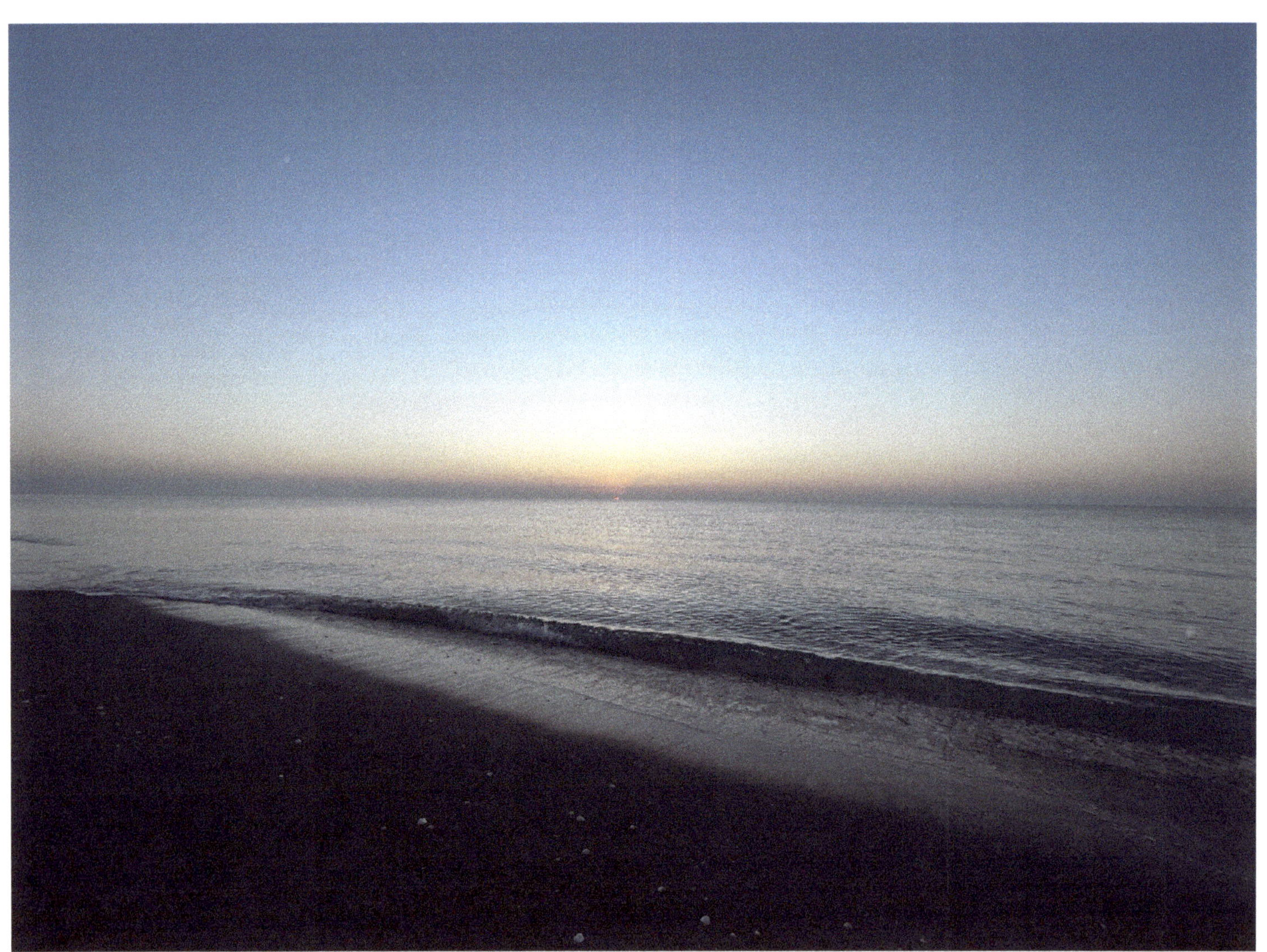

Stillness

The stillness of a new day with all it has to offer.
Leaving behind all the worries of yesterday.
A second chance to love, forgive, connect, and live.
A fresh start with a new perspective.
A moment to pause in gratitude.
Seeing, feeling, hearing, and breathing in all the wonders of being alive.

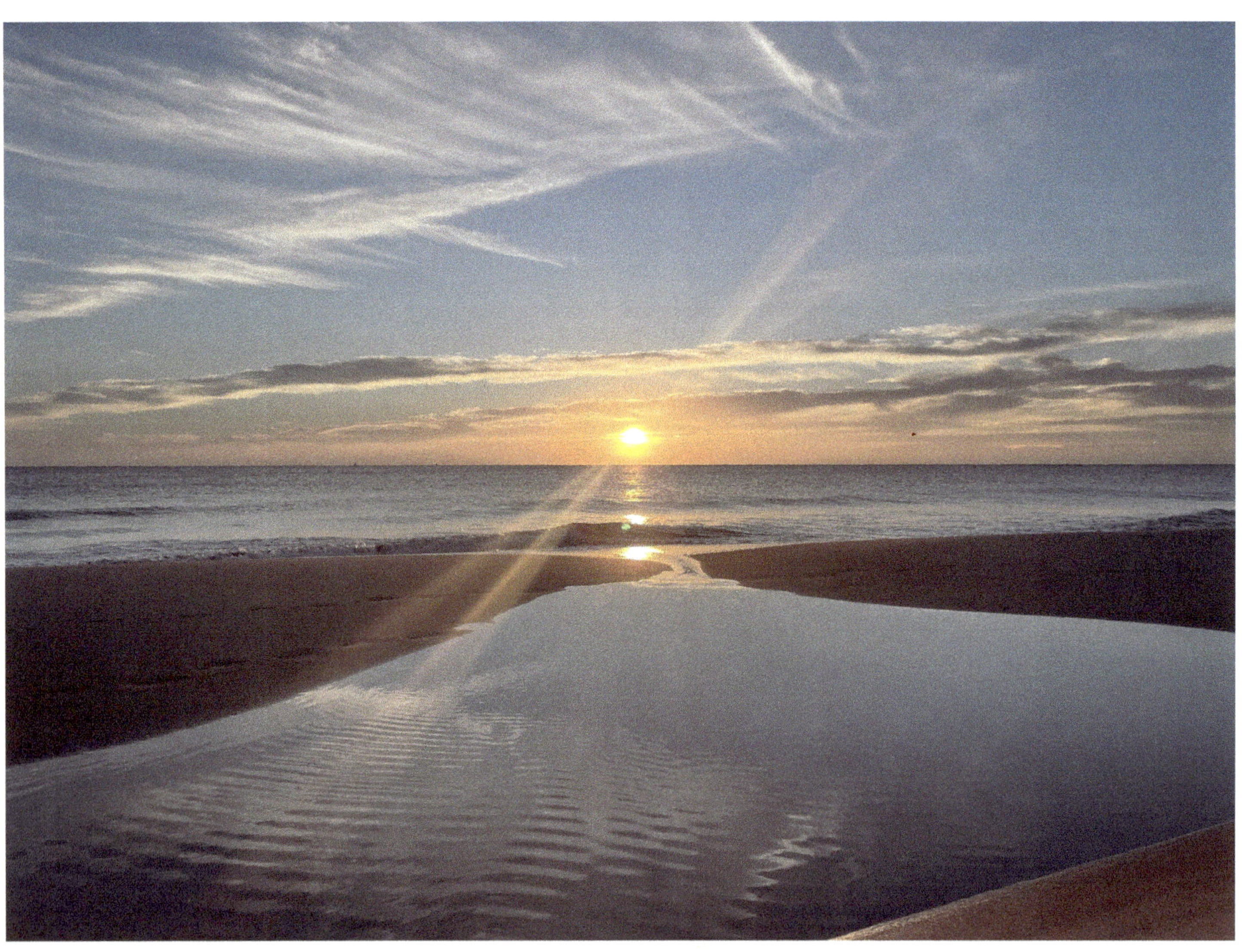

Just in Time

Find the time.
Time after time.
Make the time.
Be on time.
Do you have time?
Time keeps ticking.
I need more time.
Time passes by.
I'll make the time.
Just in time.

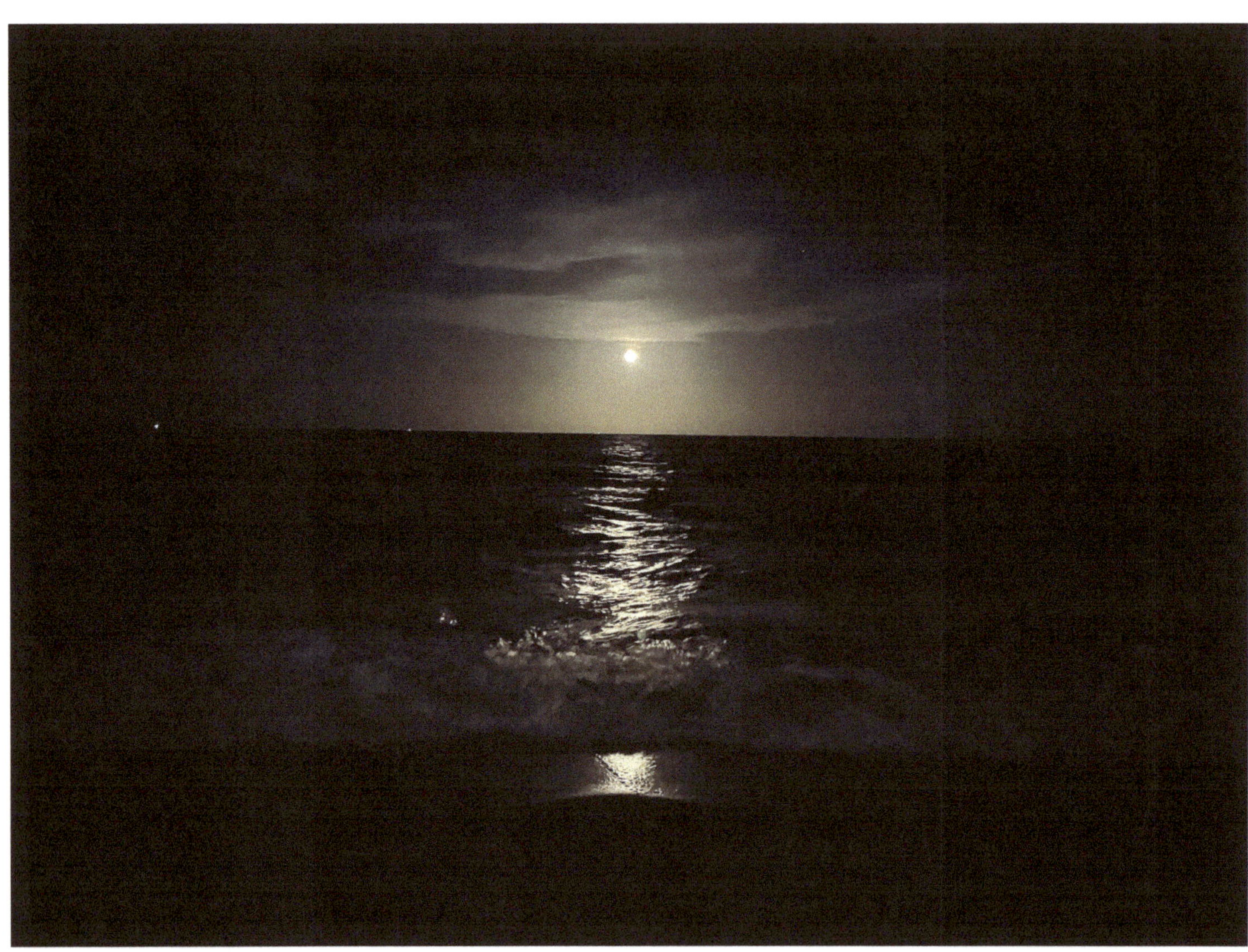

The Ripple Effect

Rushing in. Pulling out.
Cascading all around.
Looking out. Seeing the effects.
Of thoughts, of actions far and wide
Like moonbeams dancing on the tide,
Thoughts and actions, far and wide,
With every choice that you decide
Our influence can reach the other side,
Spreading ripples of love, day and night.

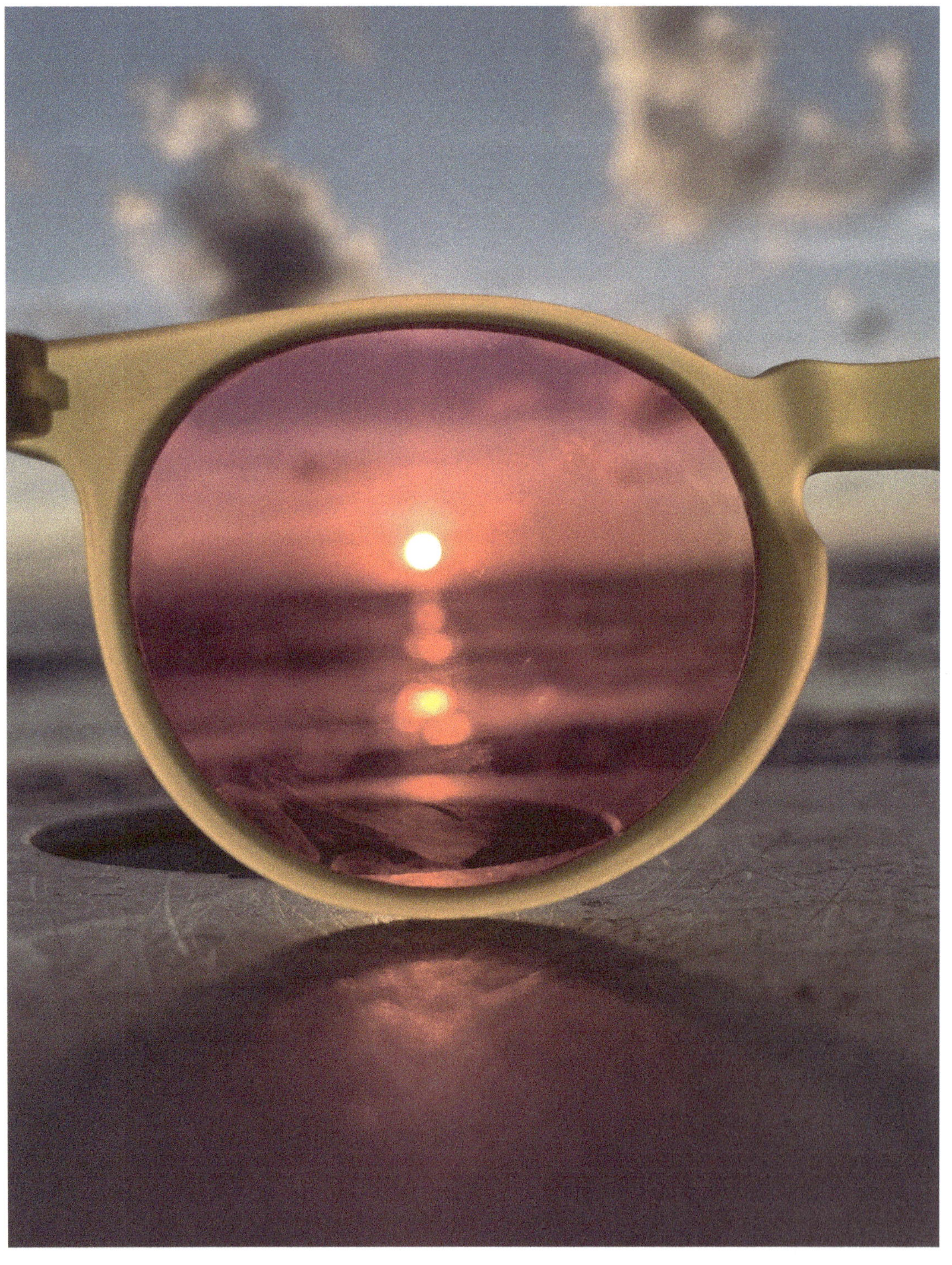

See the World Through Rose Colored Glasses

The lens of life, which one is yours?
Dark or light
Brown or yellow
Blue or rainbow
Which one is yours?
The lens of life.
How is yours?
Blurry or crisp
Scratched or repaired
Faded or bright
The lens of life.
The choice is yours.

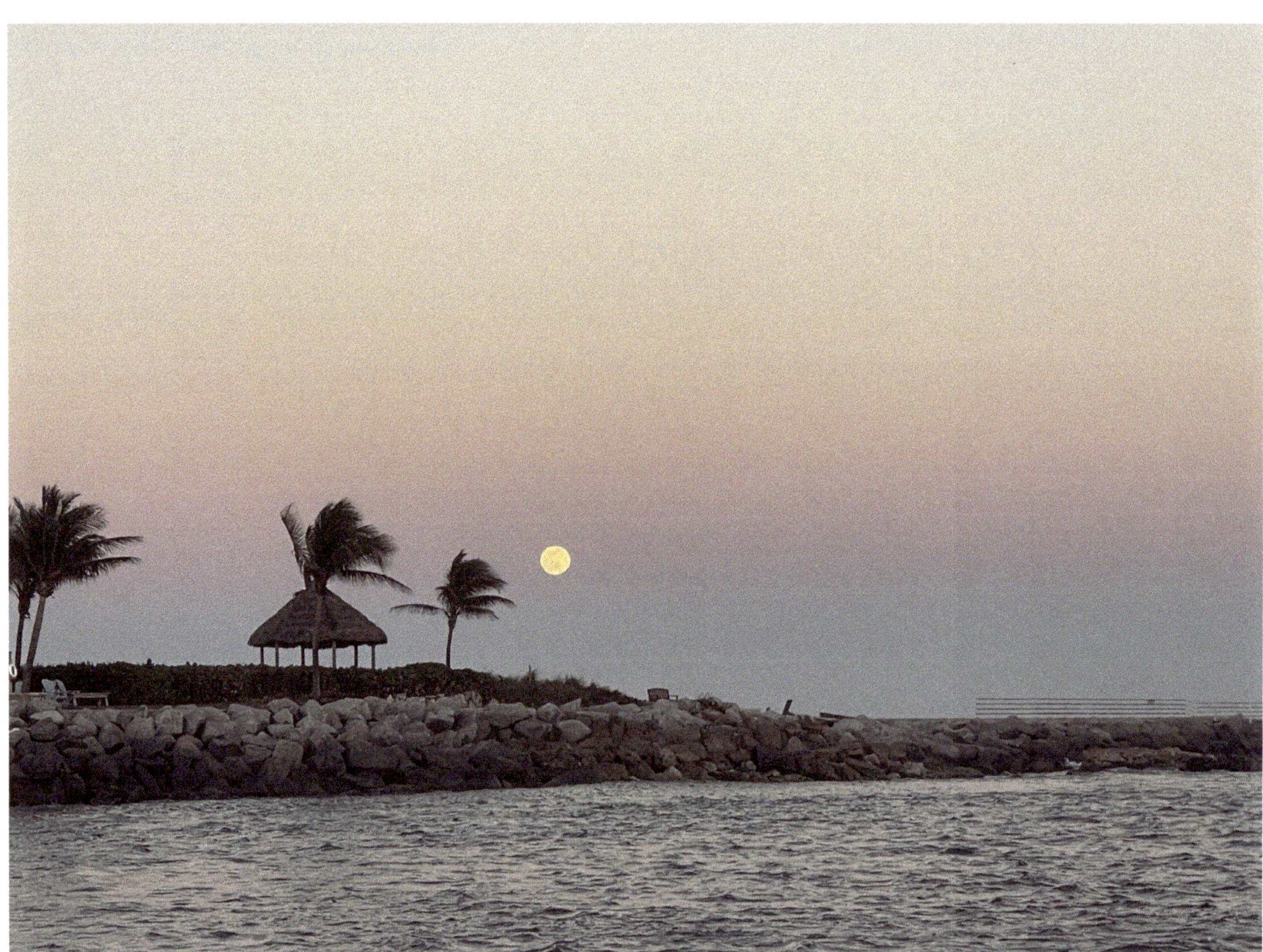

Gratitude

For health, wealth, breath, and death
For the moon, the stars, the sun, and the clouds
For family, friends, colleagues, and strangers
For all that I am, and all that I am not, and all that I can be.
I am Thankful.

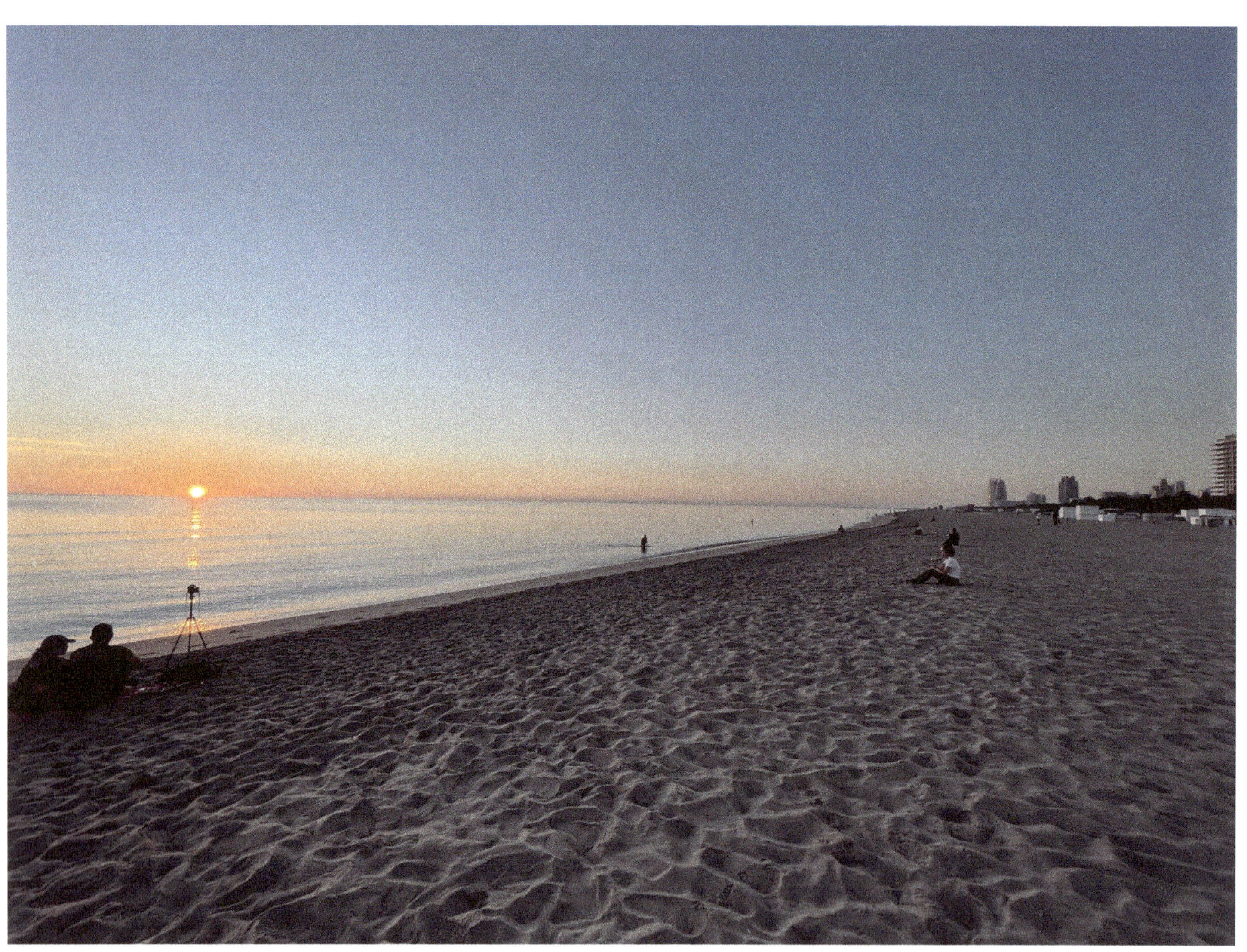

Sunrise Strangers

Watching and waiting for the day to begin
As the sun slowly rises and warms them within.
Stories untold, contemplated inside.
Each one holding something to hide.
Connected somehow through the rising sun.
Water glistens, light shines on each one.
A fleeting gaze opens doors to their soul,
As we all look out on the beauty to behold.

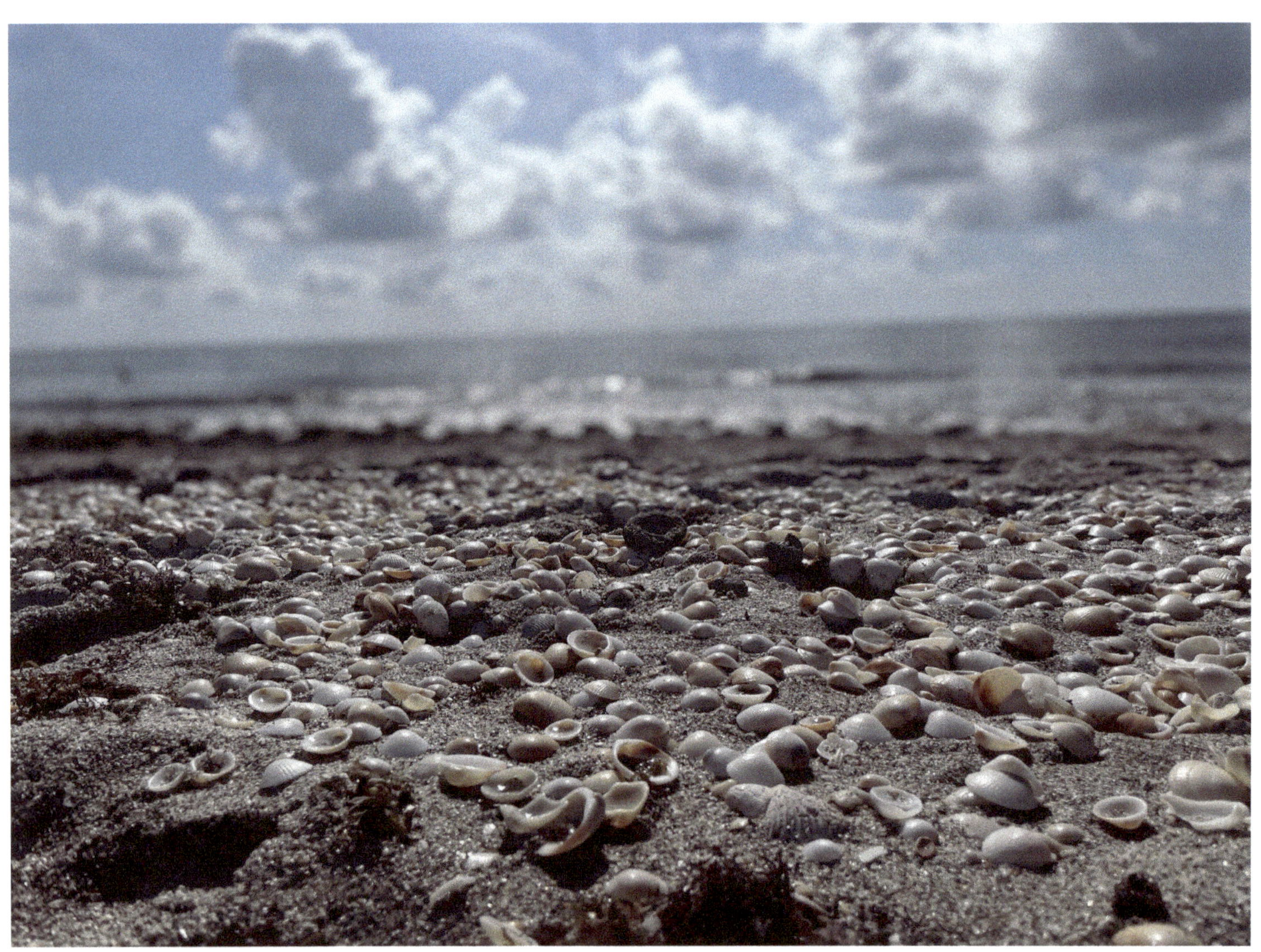

Remember

Remember me, remember you, remember who? What will I do?
Forget this, forget that, forget to do, who are you?
Losing me, losing you, losing it all, don't let me fall.
Always faith, always love, always light, never give up the fight.

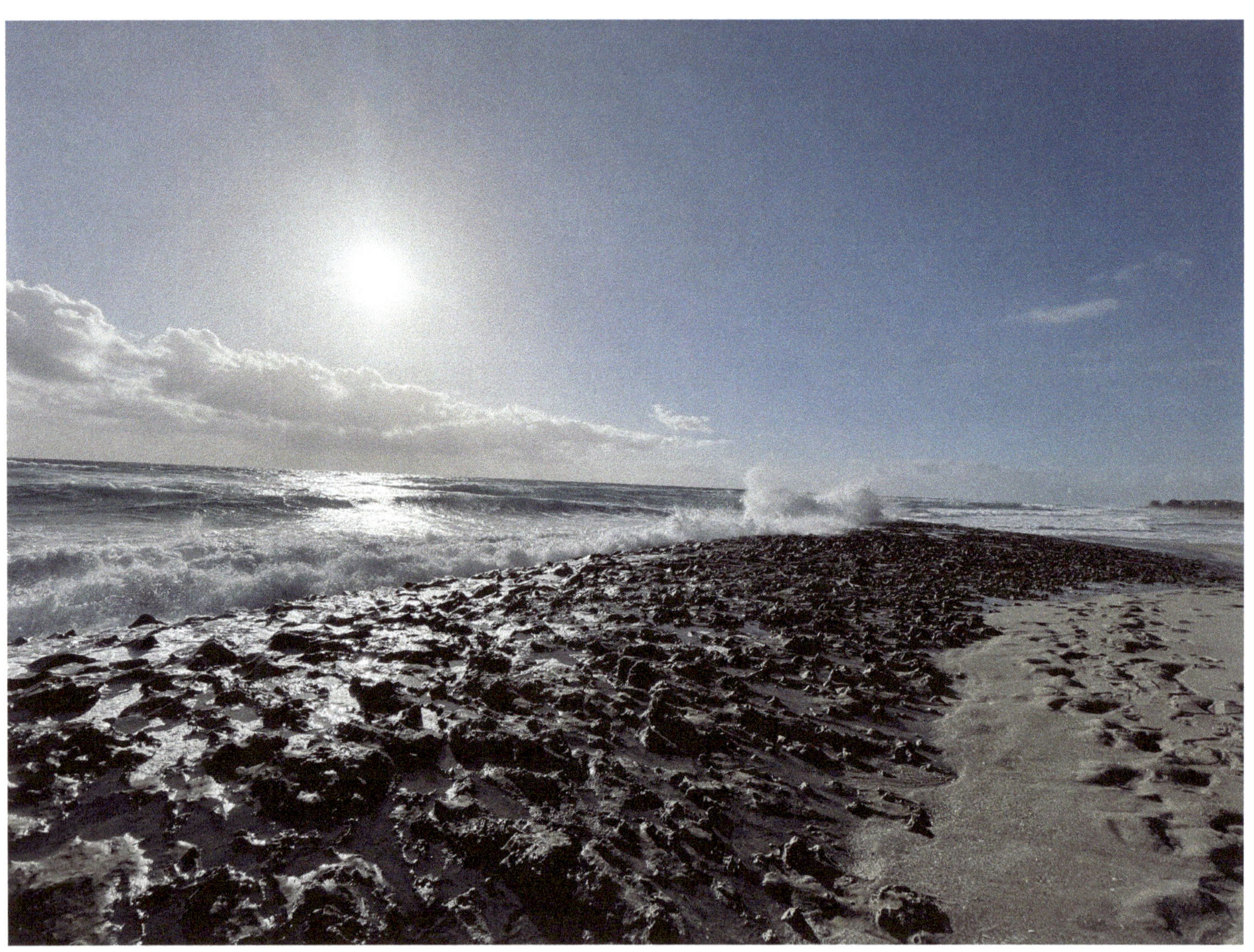

Ponder

As waves crash on the shore and the sun rises in the distance, they gather.
Questions that may never be answered. Needing hope and love and peace and purpose.
Is it the beginning or the end?
Is it over or only just begun?
Where do the truths lie?
Down beneath the ocean floor or high above light years across the sky.
Pondering deeply with feet grounded in the sand.

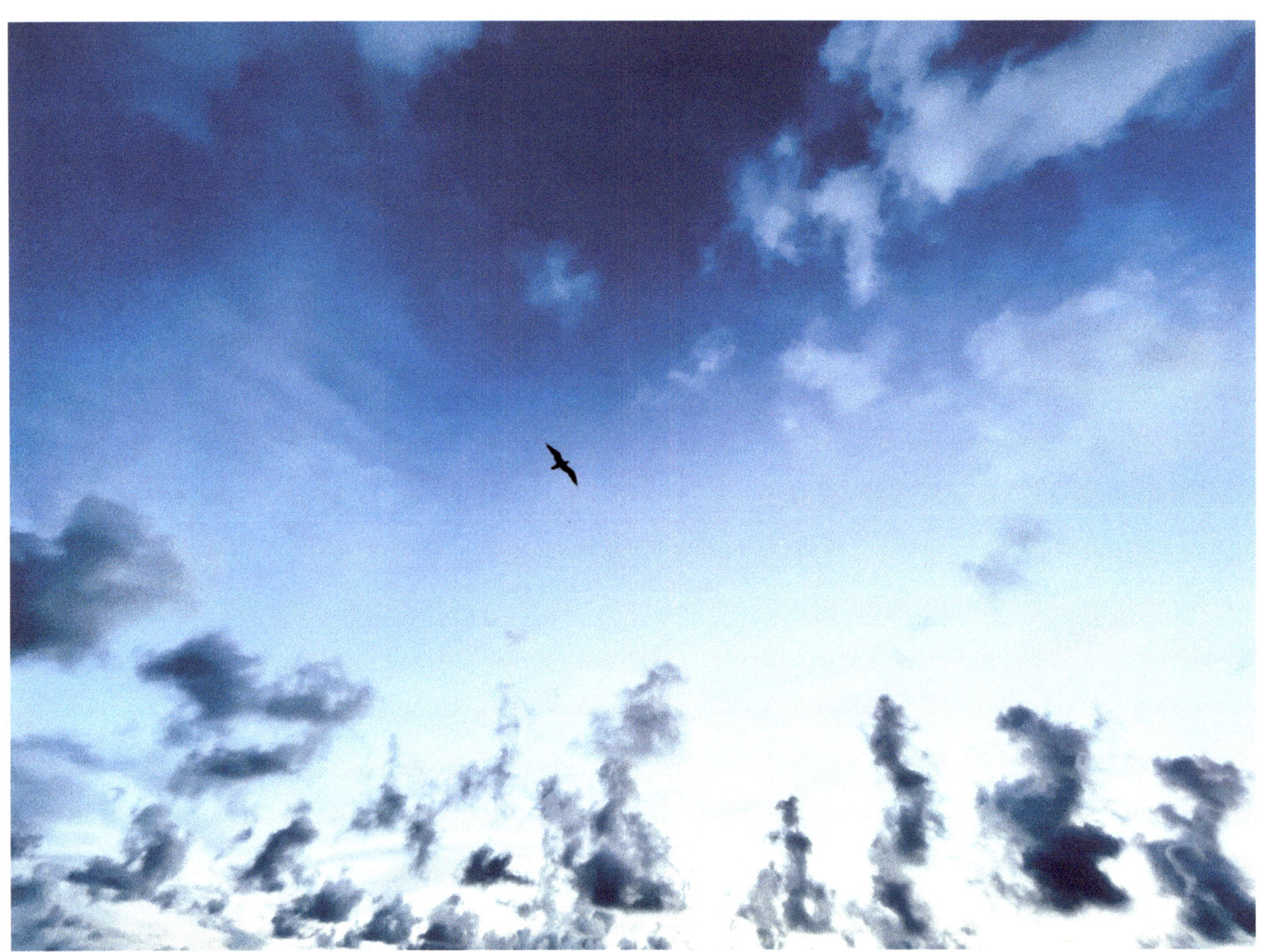

Come Home

Looking out the window, rain comes falling down.
Wondering if you're coming home, I'm tired of being alone.
The days grow long, the nights are eternity.
Without you next to me, my heart is empty.
Come home to me. Stand by my side.
Walk hand in hand, go for a ride.
Come home to me. I miss you so.
I love you.
I need you.
I want you.
Come home.

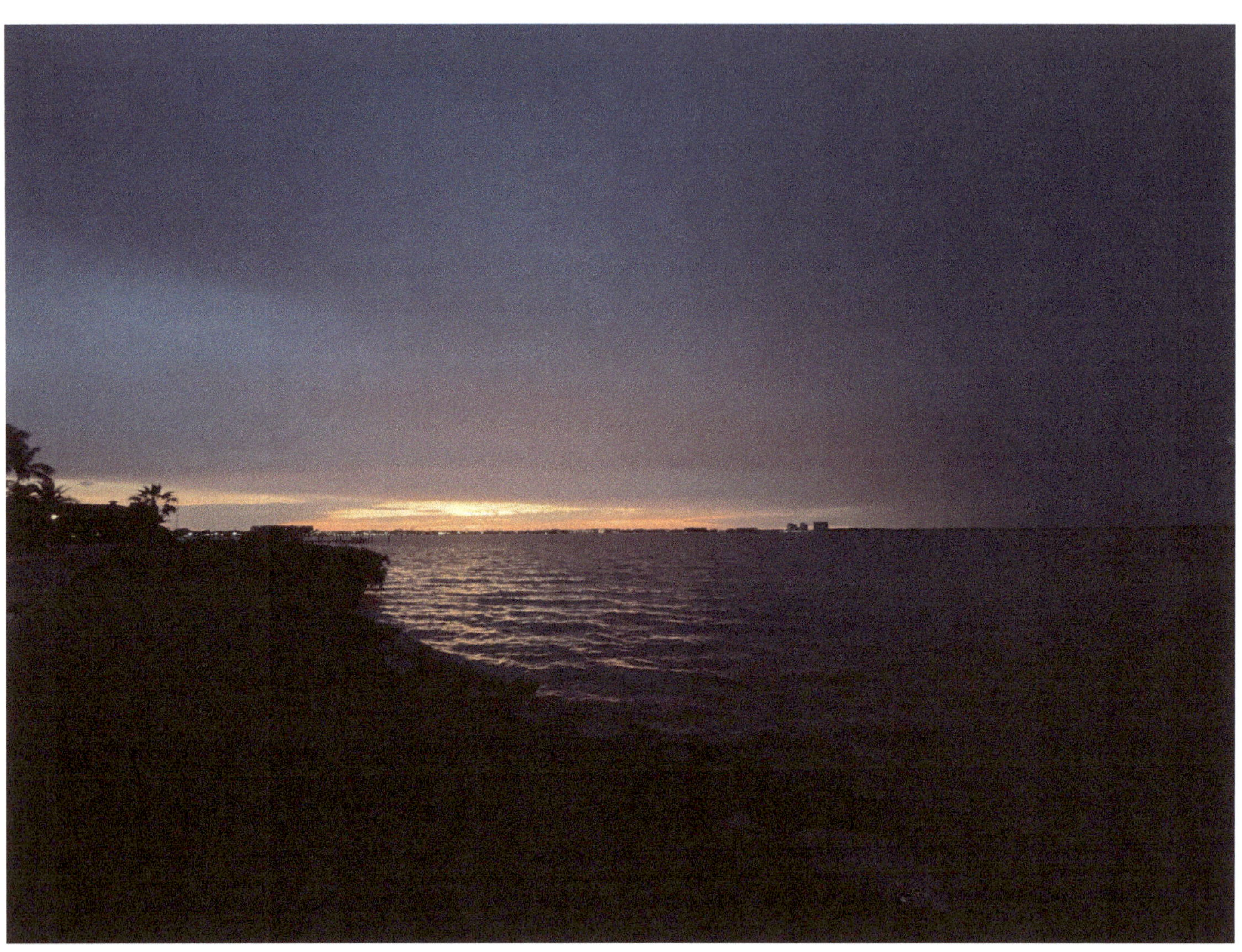

Fire Burning as Night Falls

A moment unfolds,
Where storm clouds gather, and sunlight molds.
The burning sunset breaks through the night,
Casting its flames, a contrasting sight.

Time passes by, as shadows converge,
Yet the bright rays persist, refusing to submerge.
Amidst the darkness, a glimmer of hope,
A symbol of resilience, a way to cope.

The storm clouds may loom, with thunder's roar,
But the sun's gentle glow endures evermore.
A reminder that even in the darkest hour,
There's a flicker of light, a source of power.

This moment a symbol of life's constant dance,
A reminder to seize every fleeting chance.
In the face of contrast, both bright and dark,
We find strength, authenticity, and embark.
For in the struggle, a deeper truth lies,
A sincere reminder that hope never dies.

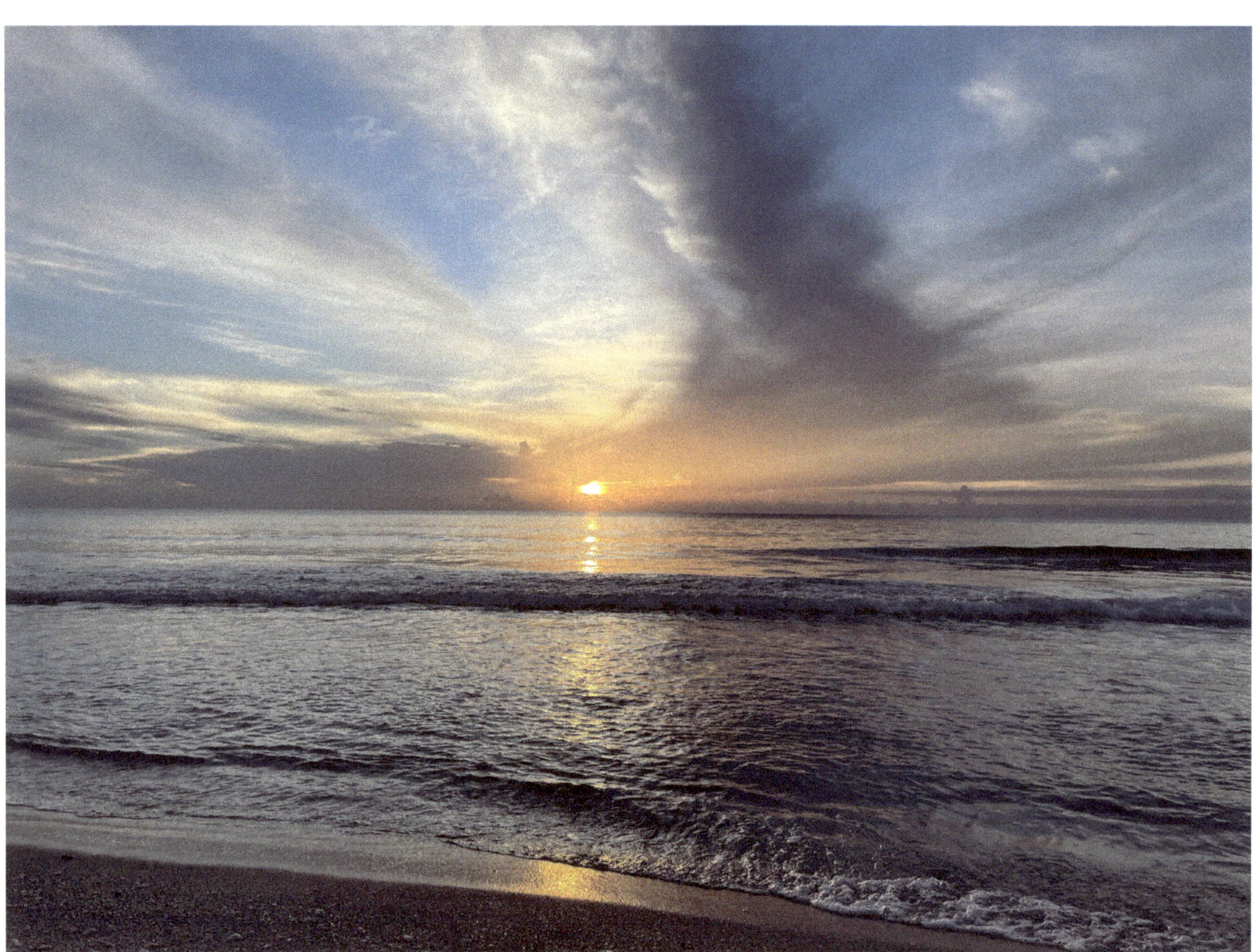

Sunrise Color Canvas

Sunrise paints the sky.
Foggy clouds form a canvas,
Where the sun paints its glory.
Time passes in hues.
As the sun rises,
Colors blend in the distance
Forming hopes for the new day as
Time passes with grace.

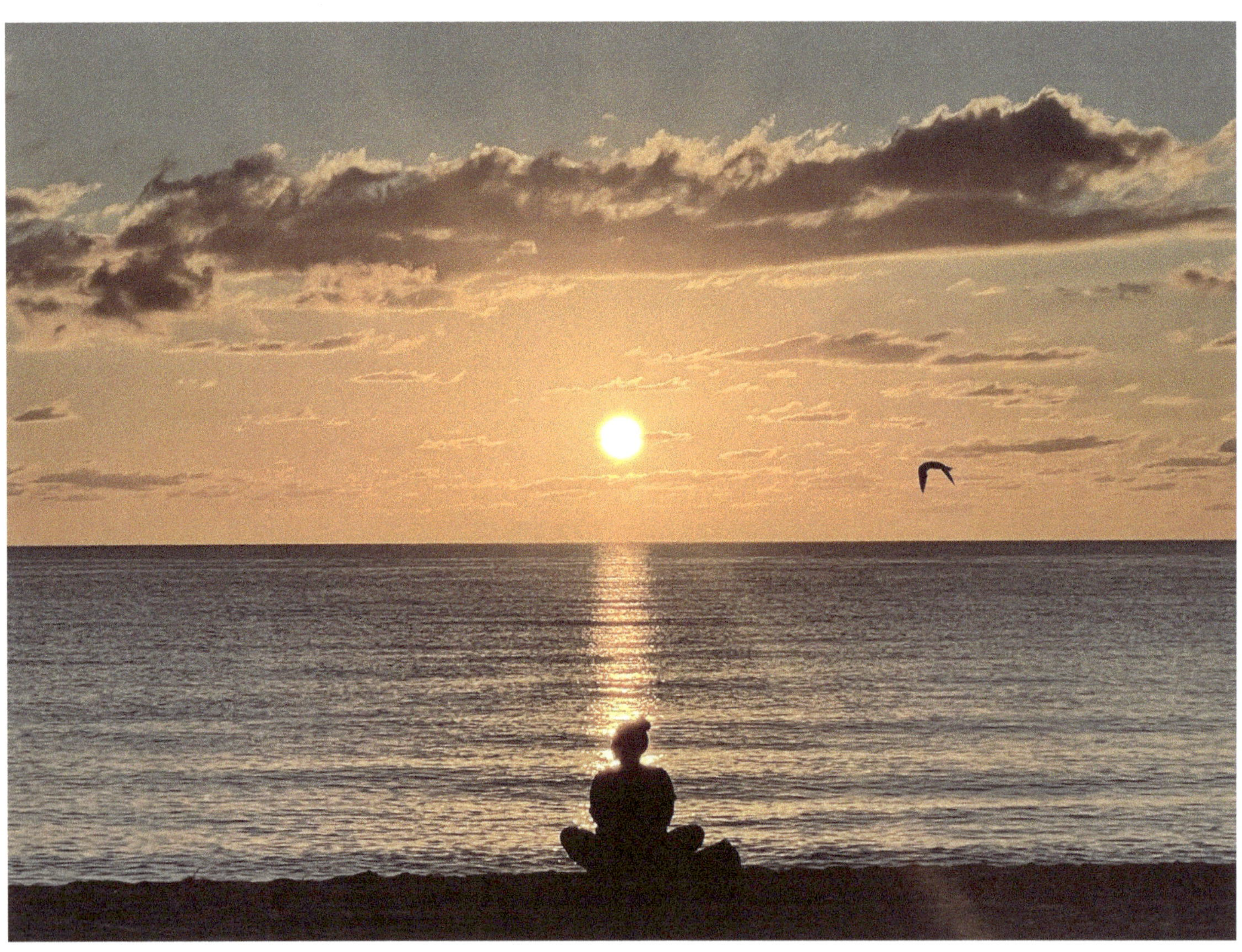

Meaningful Life

Let me live my life so that it has meaning.
Let me live my life with feeling.
Let me live my life to serve.
Let me live my life and observe.
Let me live my life as it was meant to be.
Let me live my life so that others can see,
The meaning of life.
Remind me why I came here.
Remind me there's a reason.
Remind me through the sunrise.
Remind me with each sunset.
Remind me every day,
The meaning of life.

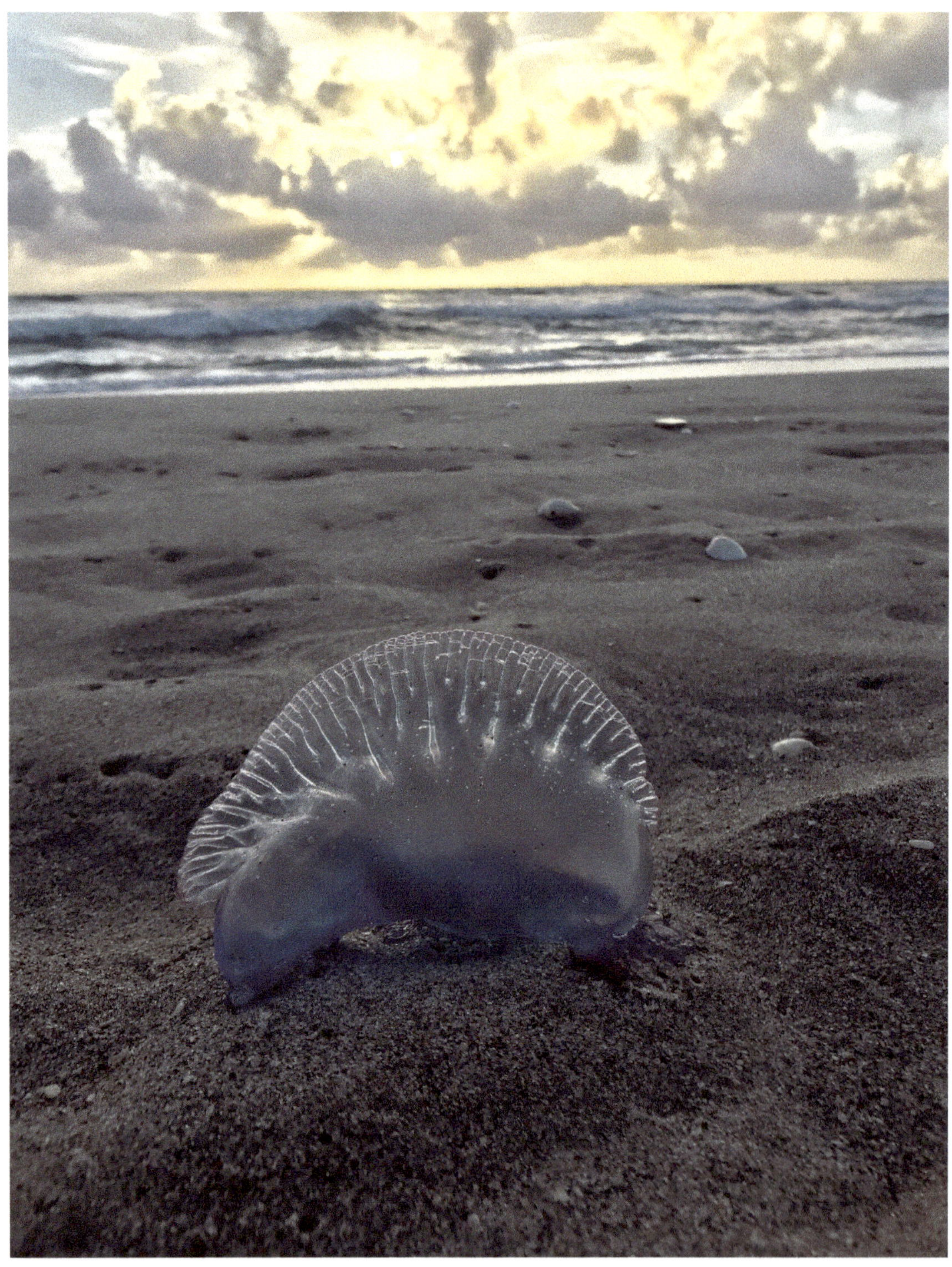

Stuck

It is in your mind, it is in your soul.
How you see the world, is in your control.
Whatever happens time and again,
Your thoughts will guide you,
Through it all until the end.
In letting go, you'll find the key,
To unlock the door and set yourself free.
From chains that bind, from fears that hold
Embrace the journey, let life unfold.

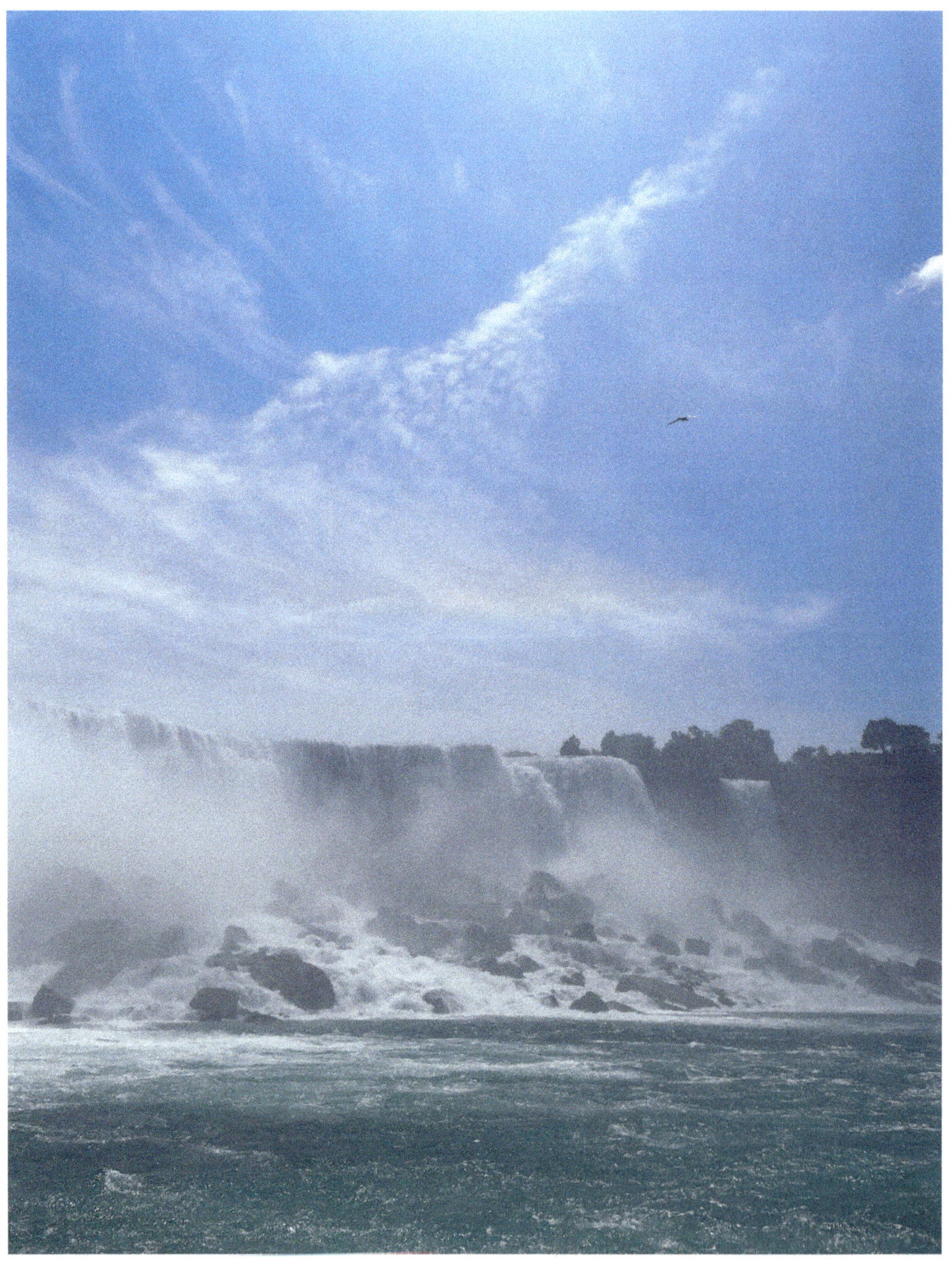

Niagara Rainbow

Colors mark the sky.
Bird flying high.
Water rushing by.
Wondering how and why.
Beauty all around.
Majestic falls go down.
Peace that all have found.
Hearing roaring sounds.
Mist giving a chill.
Feeling such a thrill.
Souls begin to fill.
Time stands still.

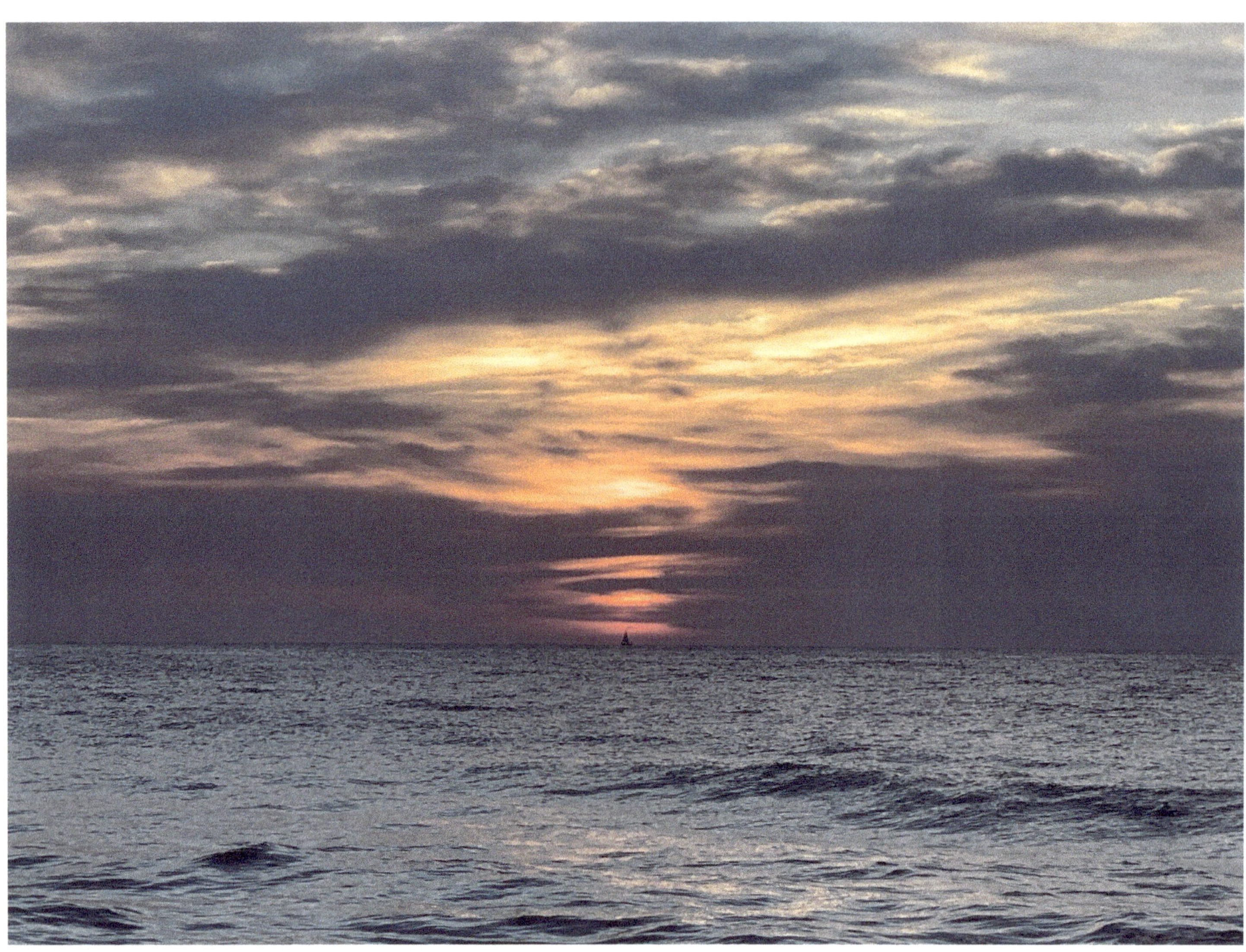

Colors In The Wind

Light that can bend.
Colors that blend.
Beauty one can't comprehend.
A way to fend.
Love to send.
More life to tend.
More love to lend.
Hearts will mend.
You are my friend.
Let yourself transcend.
Don't ever end.

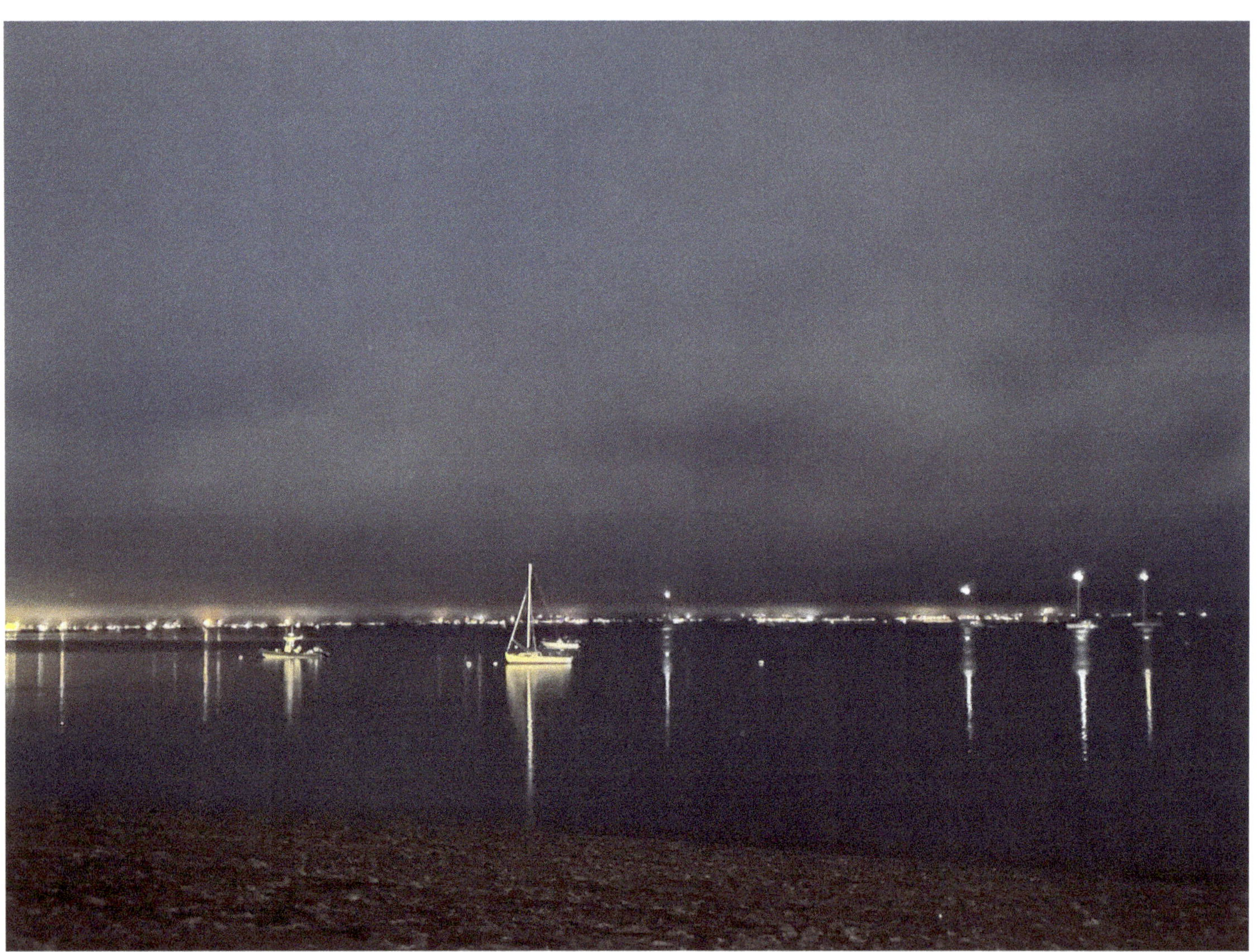

Pressure

Pressure building with dreams seemingly out of reach.
Waiting and wondering if somehow, someway the day will come.
Moving about, bouncing here and there.
Trying to find the moment that may never arrive.
Time ticking faster and faster with each passing day.
Creating a distance too far to reach.
Wanting to turn back the hands of time, have a chance to do it all again.
But time slowly slips away, the dream fading faster.
Everyone watching and wondering will it ever come to be.
Keeping it all bottled up inside so that no one will see.
Don't give up. Don't let go. Tomorrow brings a new day.

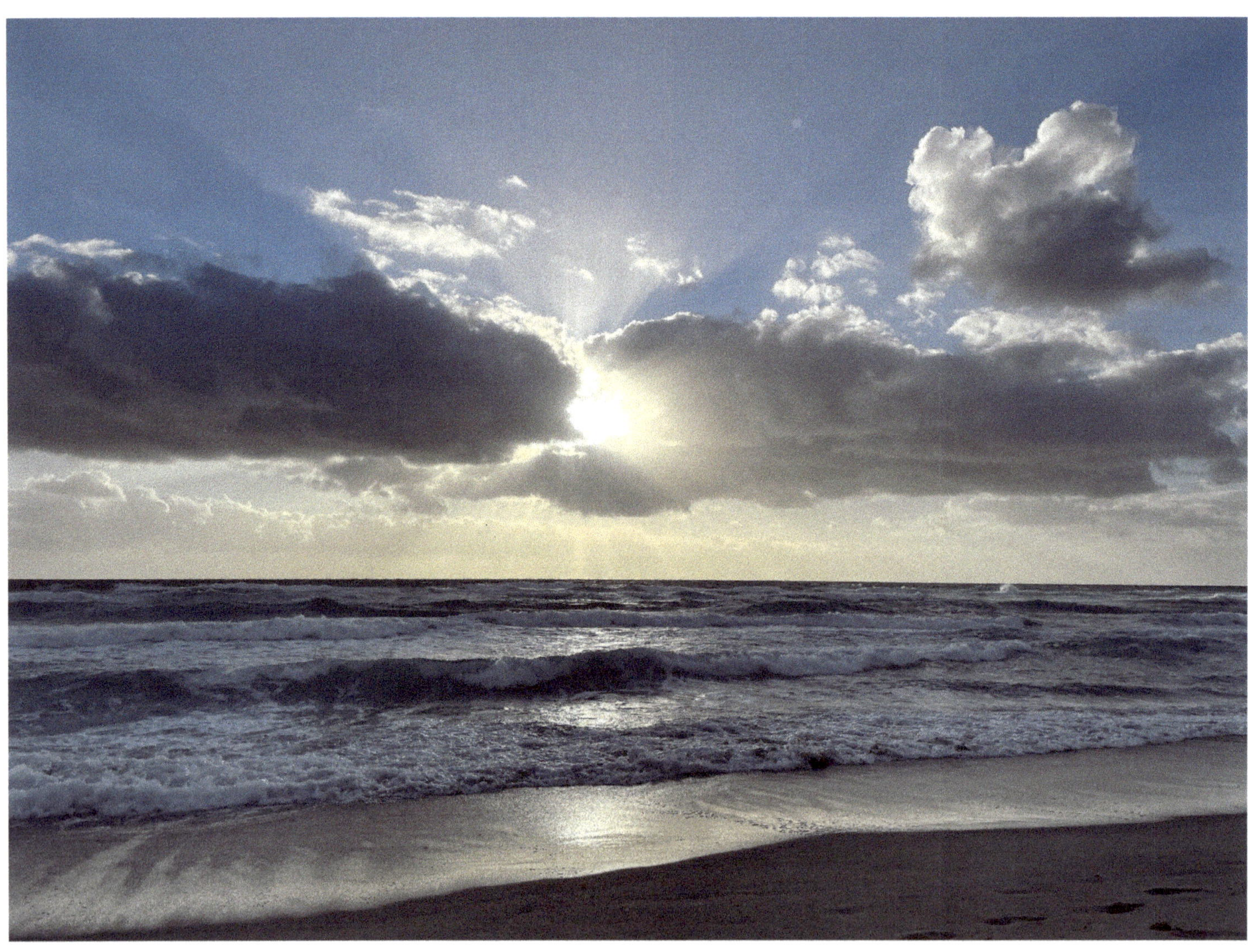

Connected

You are me and I am you.
We are they and they are you.
As we are one under the sun.
Beyond the stars from near or far.
Connected to each other,
Through light and love in all you do.

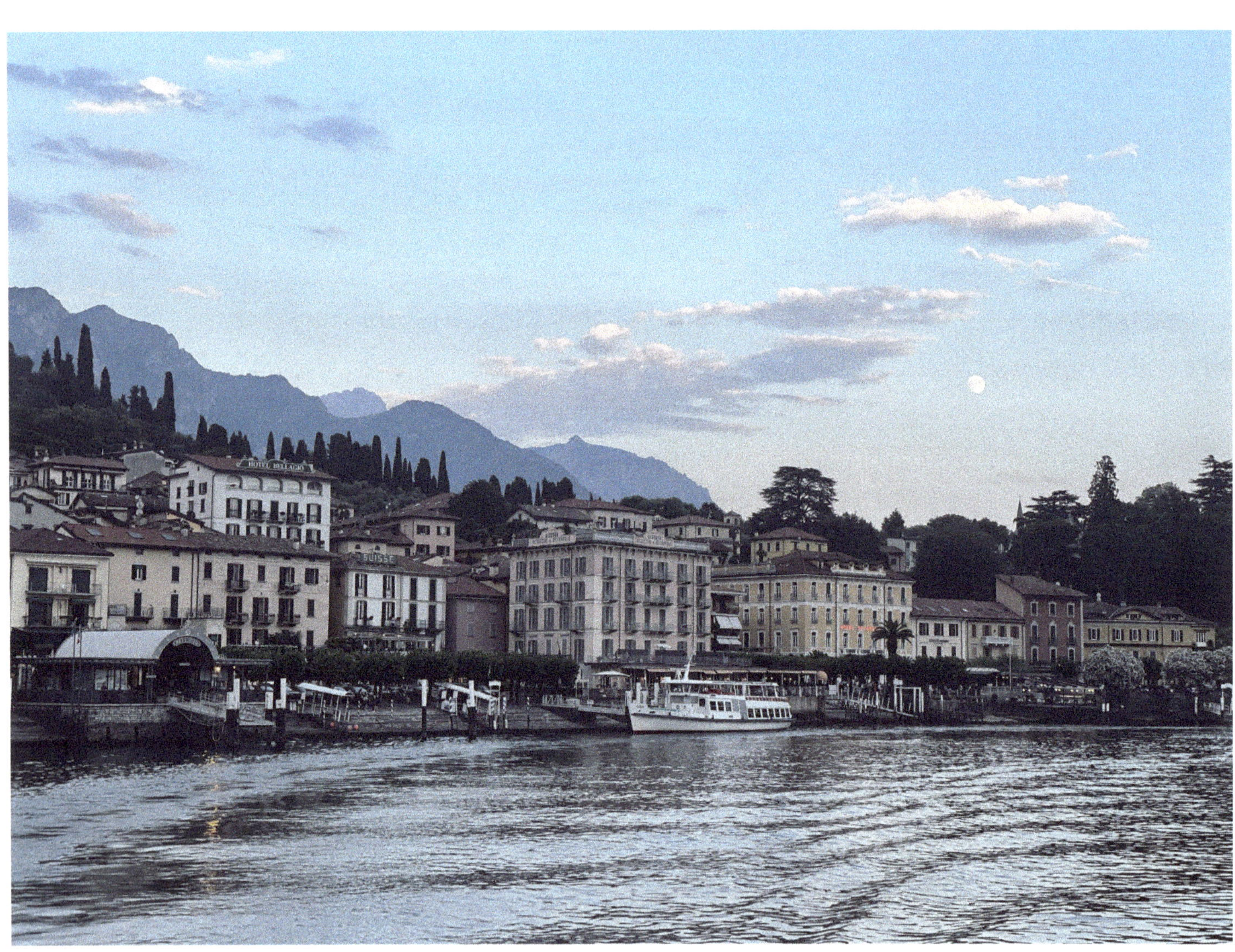

Moonrise

Standing in silence seeking serenity in the sky
as she shifts star bound over the sea.
A beacon of light in the darkness
illuminating the path set forth for you.
Glistening with ripples in motion
with promises of a new day to come.

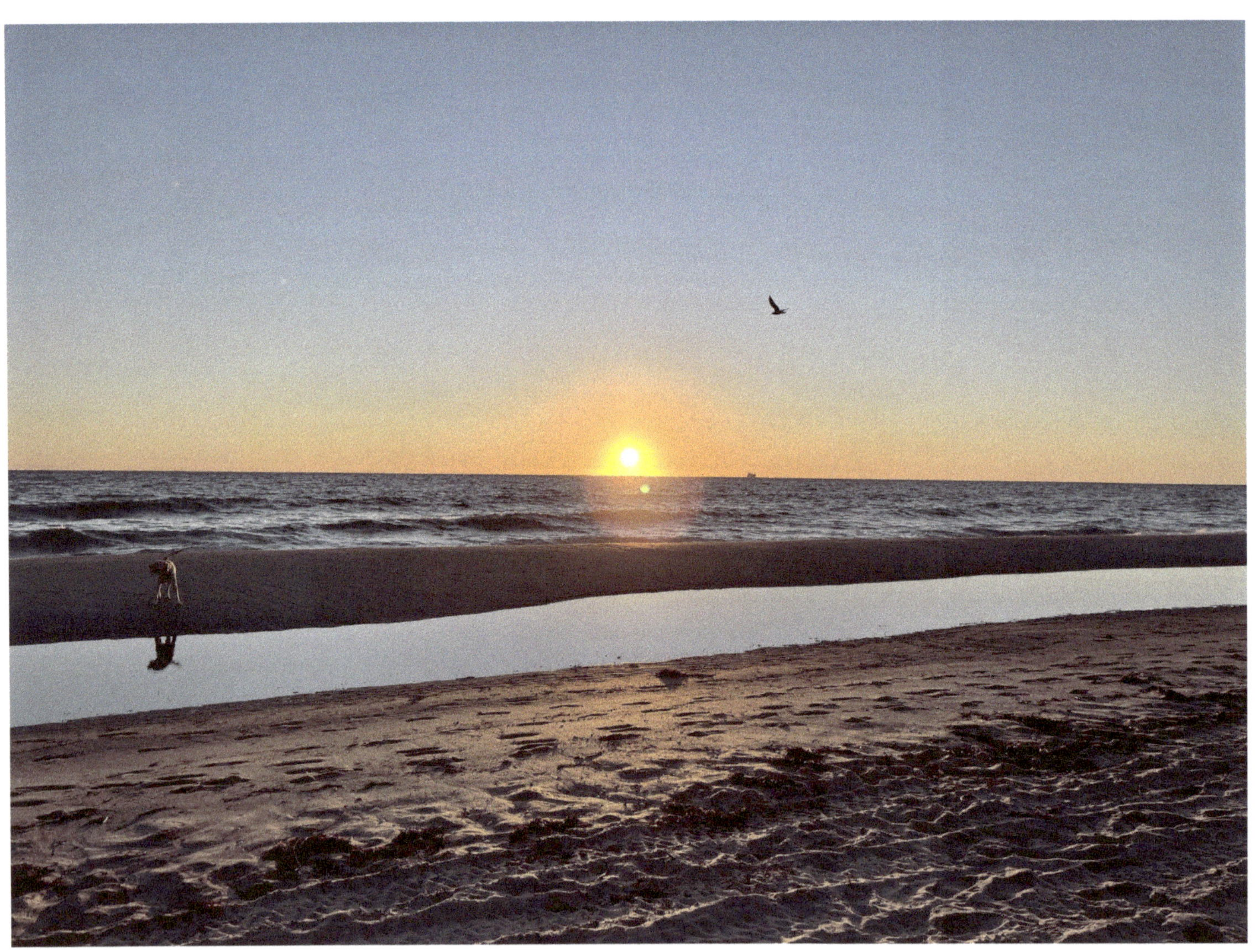

Morning Walks on the Beach

Sand creeps in your toes.
Waves rush at your feet.
Mist cools your legs.
Sun shines on your chest.
Strangers pass through your soul.
Birds fly by your eyes.
Wind blows in your hair.
Reflections weigh down your thoughts.
Gratitude fills your mind.

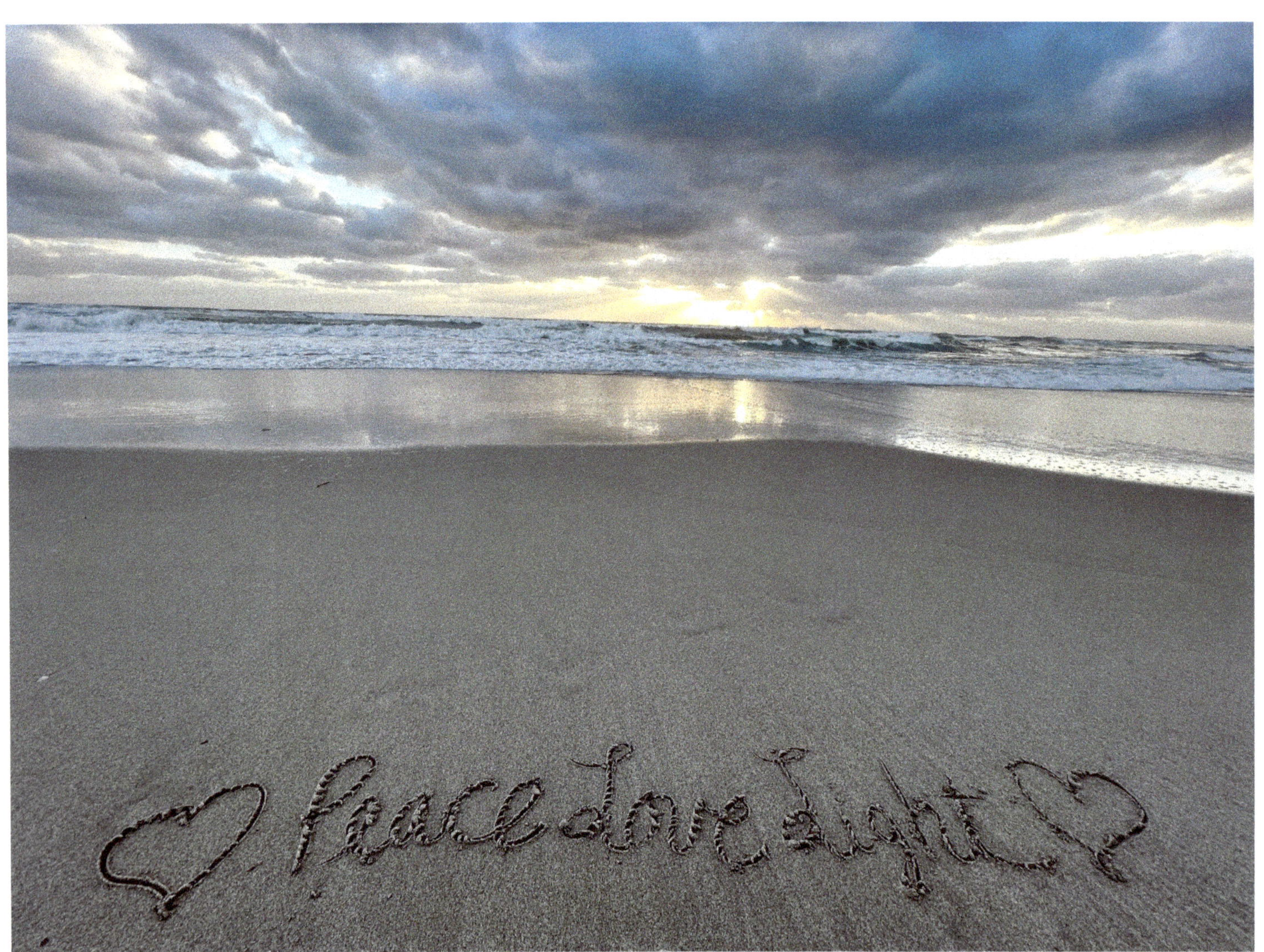
peace love light

The Light

The light has returned, peering in ever slowly as the clouds dissipate.
Pushing through, holding strong, knowing darkness was only its absence,
And now resuming what it was meant to be.
Warming the living and shining light on the dead
So we never forget the meaning ahead.
To give love and get love.
To feel joy and give joy.
The moment is here.
Take a breath.
Feel the light.
Hold on tight.

About the Author

Capturing life's essence through words and lenses, Marlene Sotelo, a passionate observer of life's wonders, is a multi-talented artist whose creativity knows no bounds. With her first published book, a captivating blend of photography and poetry, Marlene invites readers on a heartfelt journey through the depths of her soul.

Born with an innate love for nature, Marlene's affinity for the ocean runs deep within her veins. Its rhythmic waves and vast expanse have always held a special place in her heart. Through her lens, she immortalizes the ever-changing tides, capturing the essence of the ocean's allure. Each photograph carries the weight of her reverence, conveying a profound connection with the natural world. Her adoration extends beyond the ocean's embrace, finding solace in the ethereal beauty of sunrises and sunsets.

Marlene's lens becomes a conduit, skillfully freezing moments where the sun's golden rays paint the sky. With her photographs, she encapsulates the awe-inspiring transition from darkness to light, a metaphor for life's transformative journey. But Marlene's talents reach far beyond the realms of visual art.

For most of her career, she has dedicated herself to working with individuals with autism and other developmental disabilities. As a music therapist, teacher, and behavior analyst, she has touched countless lives, offering support, understanding, and encouragement. Her profound experiences with these extraordinary individuals have shaped her perspective and enriched her creativity.

In addition to her photography and devotion to helping others, Marlene's artistic expression manifests through her original songs. She has written and recorded numerous pieces, each one bearing her soulful melodies and heartfelt lyrics. Her music, like her photography, encapsulates the essence of living and loving, resonating with the depths of human emotions.